English Language Learning

Name _____ Date _____

Lesson 21
- ☐ Phonics Word Reading
- ☐ Spelling
- ☐ Sight Words
- ☐ Story 21 ◆ Samuel
- ☐ Vocabulary

Lesson 22
- ☐ Phonics Word Reading
- ☐ Spelling
- ☐ Sight Words
- ☐ Story 22 ◆ King Saul
- ☐ Vocabulary

Lesson 23
- ☐ Phonics Word Reading
- ☐ Spelling
- ☐ Sight Words
- ☐ Story 23 ◆ David as a Young Man
- ☐ Vocabulary

Lesson 24
- ☐ Phonics Word Reading
- ☐ Spelling
- ☐ Sight Words
- ☐ Story 24 ◆ David as King
- ☐ Vocabulary

Lesson 25
- ☐ Phonics Word Reading
- ☐ Spelling
- ☐ Sight Words
- ☐ Story 25 ◆ King Solomon
- ☐ Vocabulary

Lesson 26
- ☐ Phonics Word Reading
- ☐ Spelling
- ☐ Sight Words
- ☐ Story 26 ◆ Naaman
- ☐ Vocabulary

Lesson 27
- ☐ Phonics Word Reading
- ☐ Spelling
- ☐ Sight Words
- ☐ Story 27 ◆ Jonah
- ☐ Vocabulary

Lesson 28
- ☐ Phonics Word Reading
- ☐ Spelling
- ☐ Sight Words
- ☐ Story 28 ◆ The Fiery Furnace
- ☐ Vocabulary

Lesson 29
- ☐ Phonics Word Reading
- ☐ Spelling
- ☐ Sight Words
- ☐ Story 29 ◆ Daniel and the Den of Lions
- ☐ Vocabulary

Lesson 30
- ☐ Phonics Word Reading
- ☐ Spelling
- ☐ Sight Words
- ☐ Story 30 ◆ Esther
- ☐ Vocabulary

© Copyright 2017 by John and Jan Walsh ◆ This edition printed August 2019
Published by BibleTelling ◆ 2905 Gill St. ◆ Bloomington, IL 61704, U.S.A. ◆ Cover Design by Joe Horine
To contact the author, email: info@LanguageOlympics.org

Tutor Guide

Overview
- This course is designed for one-on-one tutoring. Anyone who speaks and reads English can serve as a tutor to help an ESL student.
- Each Language Olympics lesson centers around an Old Testament story.
- The Phonics, Sight Words, and Stories in the lessons are available as Audio Assist files on our website, LanguageOlympics.org and in a BibleTelling app. (Instructions at the end of this page)
- Before starting, students are pre-tested. Contact the BibleTelling office for information about the free pretest that goes with this course.

Supplies
- Pencils for all written activities
- Separate paper for spelling practice and test
- Half-sheet of dark paper to help keep student's eyes on each line of text
- Yellow highlighter for marking sight words in the story
- Green pen for tutor signatures
- Bilingual dictionary or electronic translator
- Scripture text in the student's native language

Phonics Word Reading
- This page deals with the sounds of words. It is important for practicing pronunciation.
- Students don't have to know the meanings of all the words on the Phonics page; but if they are curious, look up words using a bi-lingual dictionary or electronic translator. Some students will want to write the word in their language next to each English word.
- Your student may need to hear you say the word first. The tutor reads the word, and the student "echoes". Then the student reads the words alone.

Spelling
- The spelling words are taken from the phonics page. These are selected, based on their frequency of use in everyday language. It is important for the student to know the meaning of the spelling words.
- The student first reads the list of spelling words and then reads each word and spells it aloud.
- Word Meanings: Using a bilingual dictionary or electronic translator, help your student find the meaning of each word in their own language and write it on the line next to the word.
- Finally, the student draws lines to match words with sentences and fills in each blank with the correct English word.
- Spelling (page 2): Match words and pictures.
- Spelling Practice and Test: The tutor dictates the words, and the student writes them. Work on this for a reasonable length of time. If the student is having trouble with certain words, underline them and make a note to review next time.

Sight Words
- Students must learn to instantly recognize the *sight words*. These often don't sound the way they are spelled. Students don't have to spell the sight words — just be able to read them and know the meanings. This prepares learners to read and understand the stories.
- Students will write the meaning of each sight word in their native language.

Use Sight & Spelling Words
The student reads the sentences aloud and matches each one with the best picture. If any of the sentences seem confusing, explain the meanings as needed.

Reading the Story
- Using the Scripture references provided, find the story in the student's native language. You may find the text online and print a copy. The student may also read it on a computer or smartphone – or listen to an audio version.
- Using the list on the left side of the page, the student highlights each word where it appears in the story.
- **Listen to the Story in English:** The tutor reads the story, and the student follows along in the text. OR-the student listens to the story in the Audio Assist files (recordings) on LanguageOlympics.org or in the BibleTelling app.
- The student then reads the entire story aloud with as much help from the tutor as needed.

Story Review and Telling the Story
- The student uses words from the boxes to fill in the blanks.
- Then the student reads the sentences aloud.
- Finally, the student tells the story in his/her own words.

Vocabulary
- The student draws lines to match words and pictures.

Two Options for Listening to Words and Stories

1) Language Olympics website
- Go to LanguageOlympics.org. Look under Tutor and Student Resources. Find English as a Second Language. Click on the green Audio Assists button.
- Choose a lesson and click to hear:
    - Phonics Word Reading
    - Sight Word Reading
    - Story Reading

2) BibleTelling app
- Go to the app store and download the free BibleTelling app. It has a white background and red letters BT.
- Open the app. At the bottom menu bar, select the icon for BibleTelling (two arrows pointing inward).
- Select the light purple ESL box.
- Choose Audio Assists. This takes you to the audio recordings. Choose a lesson and click to hear:
    - Phonics Word Reading
    - Sight Word Reading
    - Story Reading

Lesson 21
Phonics Word Reading

Words having ch nch tch

☐ Practice reading the phonics words until you have mastered them.

Section 1 — Words beginning with ch

chat	chin	chip	chop	chum	cheer
chain	change	chase	chance	cheap	cheat
chest	cheese	choose	chose	chosen	choice
chill	chair	choke	check	chick	chicken
chief	child	children	church	chapel	chapter

Section 2 — Words ending with ch

each	teach	peach	reach	beach	speech
much	such	coach	poach	roach	approach
rich	which	search	touch	bleach	preach

Section 3 — Words containing nch tch

inch	pinch	punch	lunch	bunch	bench
ranch	branch	batch	hatch	match	patch
itch	ditch	hitch	pitch	stitch	witch
catch	watch	fetch	stretch	sketch	kitchen

Section 4 — More words having ch nch tch

teacher   preacher   butcher   rancher   pitcher   catcher
armchair   wheelchair   highchair   chariot   cheerful   cheerleader
checking   checkup   checkers   paycheck

☐ My student has mastered the phonics words.   Tutor initials _____

Lesson 21 Spelling (page 1)

Words having ch nch tch

☐ Read the word list.   ☐ Read each word again and spell it aloud.

catch	chair	chance	change	check	child
children	each	kitchen	lunch	match	much
reach	rich	such	touch	watch	which

☐ Write the word in your language.   ☐ Draw lines to match the words and sentences.
☐ Use the best English word to fill in the blanks.   ☐ Read the sentences aloud.

catch _____   I hope we get a _____ to talk after the meeting.
chair _____   We need to _____ the 7:00 bus.
chance _____   They will _____ your passport before you get on the plane.
change _____   Grandpa likes to sit in a _____ outside under a tree.
check _____   Even as a _____, she liked to be with lots of people.
child _____   I'm sorry, I've had a _____ of plans. I can't come.

children _____   The teacher gave one pencil to _____ person in the class.
each _____   We will meet for _____ at noon today.
kitchen _____   He came from a large family of ten _____.
lunch _____   The thing I like best about my apartment is the _____.
match _____   How _____ does it cost to ride the bus?
much _____   I'm looking for another sock to _____ this blue one.

reach _____   She is not poor; she is _____.
rich _____   That is _____ a big, beautiful tree!
such _____   Will you _____ up and get that box from the top of the fridge?
touch _____   She will _____ the children and keep them close to the school.
watch _____   I see two bags. Do you know _____ one is yours?
which _____   Please don't _____ this book with your wet hands.

2   ☐ Checked by Tutor   Tutor initials _____

Lesson 21 Spelling (page 2)

Words having ch nch tch

☐ Read all the words.   ☐ Write the best word under each picture.

| branch | chain | cheese | chief | kitchen | touch |
| catch | chair | chick | children | matches | reach |

Spelling Test: ☐ Practice the following words until you have learned them.

1. catch
2. chair
3. chance
4. change
5. check
6. child
7. children
8. each
9. kitchen
10. lunch
11. match
12. much
13. reach
14. rich
15. such
16. touch
17. watch
18. which

☐ My student can spell these words aloud.   Tutor Initials _____

☐ My student can write these words when I read them.   Tutor Initials _____

Lesson 21 Sight Words

☐ Write the word in your language.
☐ Practice reading the words until you can pronounce them correctly.

allow	better	both
comfort	continue	drunk
enough	evil	explain
extremely	finish	heart
judgment	little	nation
notice	once	peace
positive	remember	speak
visit	voice	wrong

☐ My student can read these words and knows their meanings.   Tutor Initials _____

Lesson 21 – Use Sight & Spelling Words

☐ Read the sentences.　　☐ Draw lines to match the words and pictures.

She will speak and explain her
judgment in this case.

The little boy is reaching up
to give you his paper.

They allow their cat to sleep on their bed.

Both of the men are having lunch.

That chain was made by little children
using paper of many colors.

The boy is old enough to be a help to the old man.

Once, I had a watch just like that.

Two young girls are watching the baby sleep.

They are both asleep in that chair
that leans back almost flat.

That little puppy has his chin on the edge of the box.

It's an extremely sad day for both of them,
but he's trying to comfort her.

He is trying to explain, but they
may not allow him to finish speaking.

☐ My student can read and understand these sentences.　Tutor initials _____

Story 21 ❖ Samuel

☐ Read or listen to the story in your native language. I Samuel 1:1-28, 2:11-21, 3:1-21
☐ Find and mark the sight words in the story. ☐ Listen to the story in English.

Sight Words
allow
better
both
comfort
continued
drunk
enough
evil
explained
extremely
finished
heart
judgment
little
nation
noticed
once
peace
positive
remember
speak
visit
voice
wrong

Once there was a woman named Hannah who had no children. This made her extremely sad. Her husband loved her and tried to comfort her. He asked, "Am I not better to you than ten sons?" But that didn't help at all.

Hannah went to worship in the Tabernacle. She was crying and praying to God, "If you will give me a son, I will give him back to you and he will serve you for his whole life."

Eli, the old priest at the Tabernacle, noticed Hannah's mouth moving, but he couldn't hear her voice. He thought she was drunk.

"Oh, sir, I'm not drunk!" she explained. "I'm praying to God in my heart."

When she finished, the priest said, "Go in peace; may God answer your prayer."

About a year later, Hannah gave birth to a son and named him Samuel, a name that means 'God heard me'. When the boy was old enough, his mother brought him back to stay with Eli and help him.

She said to the priest, "Remember when I prayed for a child? God answered my prayer. Now I'm giving my son to the Lord, and he will serve God for the rest of his life." So Samuel stayed at the Tabernacle and helped the old priest. Every year Hannah came to visit and brought a new, little robe for Samuel.

Eli's two sons also worked at the Tabernacle, but they were evil. They did not obey God's laws. Eli told his sons they were doing wrong, but he didn't stop them. A prophet came to Eli with a message from God: "You have allowed your sons to do evil in my house. Therefore, they will both die in one day."

One night, while Samuel was sleeping, the Lord called out, "Samuel, Samuel."

Samuel woke up and ran to Eli. He said, "I'm here! You called me."

Eli looked at the boy. "No, Samuel. I didn't call you. Go back to bed."

As Samuel was going back to sleep, the Lord called him a second time. He got up and ran to Eli. "Here I am! You called me."

Eli said, "Son, I did not call you. Go back and lie down."

He went back and lay down. The Lord called him a third time, "Samuel, Samuel."

The third time the Lord called him, Samuel was positive he heard someone calling his name. He ran to Eli, and the old priest told him, "Go back and lie down. If you hear the voice again, say, 'Speak, Lord, for your servant is listening.'"

Samuel went back to bed. Again, the Lord called him, "Samuel, Samuel."

Samuel answered, "Speak, for your servant is listening."

The Lord said, "I am not pleased that Eli allows his sons to do evil in my house. I'm going to bring judgment on Eli and his sons."

Samuel went back to bed. In the morning, Eli asked, "Samuel, what did the Lord say to you?" Samuel was afraid to tell him the message from God, but Eli said, "Son, don't hide it from me." So Samuel told him everything.

God was with Samuel from that day on and continued to speak to him. Everything Samuel said came true. Then all the nation of Israel knew that he was a true prophet of God.

Review Story 21

Use the words in the boxes to fill in the blanks.

| better   comfort   drunk   explained   extremely   heart   noticed   Once |

1. _____ there was a woman named Hannah who had no children. This made her _____ sad. Her husband loved her and tried to _____ her. He asked, "Am I not _____ to you than ten sons?"

2. Eli, the old priest at the Tabernacle, _____ Hannah's mouth moving, but he couldn't hear her voice, so he thought she was _____.

3. "Oh, sir, I'm not drunk!" she _____. "I'm praying to God in my _____."

| both   enough   finished   little   peace   Remember   visit   evil   wrong |

4. When she _____, the priest said, "Go in _____; may God answer your prayer."

5. About a year later, Hannah gave birth to a son and named him Samuel. When the boy was old _____, his mother brought him back to stay with Eli and help him.

6. She said to the priest, "_____ when I prayed for a child? God answered my prayer. Now I'm giving my son to the Lord, and he will serve God for the rest of his life."

7. Every year Hannah came to _____ and brought a new, _____ robe for Samuel.

8. Eli's two sons also worked at the Tabernacle, but they were _____.

9. Eli told his sons they were doing _____, but he didn't stop them.

10. A prophet came to Eli with a message from God: "You have allowed your sons to do evil in my house; therefore, they will _____ die in one day."

| allows   continued   judgment   nation   positive   Speak   voice |

11. The third time the Lord called, Samuel was _____ he heard someone calling his name. He ran to Eli, and the old priest told him, "Go back and lie down. If you hear the _____ again, say, '_____, Lord, for your servant is listening.'"

12. The Lord said, "I am not pleased that Eli _____ his sons to do evil in my house. I'm going to bring _____ on Eli and his sons." In the morning, Samuel told Eli everything.

13. God was with Samuel from that day on and _____ to speak to him. Everything Samuel said came true. Then all the _____ of Israel knew that he was a true prophet of God.

Read the sentences aloud.   Tell the story in your own words.   Tutor initials _____

Vocabulary 21 – What are they thinking or saying?

☐ Read the sentences.   ☐ Draw lines to match words and pictures.

I remember when I was a young soldier.

I shouldn't allow my dog to lick my face,
but I don't mind.

I hope my teacher will notice that
I am listening better today.

When do you think our teacher will notice
that plastic frog we put in her desk?

I'm using this sign to explain what is wrong.
My throat is extremely sore,
and I have no voice today.

I wasn't sure I could reach it,
but I just made such a good catch!

I wish I could remember her name.

Right now, I can't allow my hands
to touch anything.

I learned to use chopsticks when I was little,
and I continue to use them every day.

You must allow me inside to visit.
Check my I.D., and you will see
that it matches your book.

I'm absolutely positive I can climb to the
top of that mountain.

You gave me more than enough money.
Here's your change.

☐ Checked by Tutor   Tutor initials _____

Lesson 22

Phonics Word Reading

Words with "soft c" sound
When the letter c makes the /s/ sound, we call it a "soft c"

☐ Practice reading the phonics words until you have mastered them.

Section 1 — words that begin with "soft c"

cell	celery	cent	center	cement	cemetery
cedar	ceiling	cereal	cider	cycle	cyclist
city	civic	civil	citrus	citizen	citizenship
circle	circus	certain	certainly	certificate	celebrate

Section 2 — words that end with the "soft c" sound

ace	face	lace	race	trace	brace
pace	place	palace	peace	grace	space
ice	lice	mice	nice	rice	price
vice	advice	twice	slice	spice	sacrifice
dance	chance	glance	since	once	force
ounce	pounce	bounce	announce	introduce	difference
office	notice	service	practice	piece	police
fence	evidence	sentence	audience	ambulance	experience

Section 3 — words containing the "soft c" sound

pencil	cancel	canceled	recent	receive	receptionist
acid	decide	decision	medicine	concern	concerned
concert	exercise	excite	excited	exciting	except
sincere	sincerely	success	policy	grocery	groceries
officer	vacancy	mercy	emergency	bicycle	motorcycle

☐ My student has mastered the phonics words.   Tutor initials _____

Lesson 22 Spelling (page 1)
Words with "soft c" sound

☐ Read the word list.   ☐ Read each word again and spell it aloud.

advice	center	certain	circle	circus	city
decide	office	once	peace	pencil	police
practice	price	service	since	space	twice

☐ Write the word in your language.   ☐ Draw lines to match the words and sentences.
☐ Use the best English word to fill in the blanks.   ☐ Read the sentences aloud.

advice _____   He owns a restaurant in the _____ of the city.
center _____   If you want that job, there is a _____ person you need to call.
certain _____   Can you give me some _____ about the best way to town?
circle _____   They went to the _____ and saw someone walking on a wire.
circus _____   A great number of cars come out of the _____ every evening.
city   _____   Let's sit in a _____ and talk about ideas for the party.

decide _____   She would rather work in the _____ than to be outside.
office _____   I need to _____ if I should go shopping or stay home today.
once   _____   There was a car crash, but the _____ came right away.
peace _____   He takes his dog out walking _____ a day.
pencil _____   After the war was over, they had _____ for seven years.
police _____   Use a _____ so you can erase and make changes.

practice _____   There is always good _____ at that restaurant.
price   _____   Her music teacher wants her to _____ an hour a day.
service _____   In the summer, they go swimming _____ a week.
since   _____   The _____ of fruit is high in the north where they live.
space   _____   Is there enough _____ for that truck to park here?
twice   _____   He's been living in this country _____ he was 16 years old.

☐ Checked by Tutor   Tutor initials _____

Lesson 22 Spelling (page 2)

Words with "soft c" sound

> ☐ Read all the words. ☐ Write the best word under each picture.

| celery | circle | city | dice | office | circus tent |
| cereal | pencil | dance | fence | palace | police officer |

_____ _____ _____ _____

_____ _____ _____ _____

_____ _____ _____ _____

Spelling Test: ☐ Practice the following words until you have learned them.

1. advice
2. center
3. certain
4. circle
5. circus
6. city
7. decide
8. office
9. once
10. peace
11. pencil
12. police
13. practice
14. price
15. service
16. since
17. space
18. twice

☐ My student can spell these words aloud.   Tutor Initials _____

☐ My student can write these words when I read them.   Tutor Initials _____

11

Lesson 22 Sight Words

☐ Write the word in your language.
☐ Practice reading the words until you can pronounce them correctly.

actually	almost	already
announce	attack	control
crowd	establish	fact
fail	foolish	forever
head	introduce	kingdom
member	myself	offer
shout	small	supplies
thousand	whose	yourself

☐ My student can read these words and knows their meanings.   Tutor Initials _____

Lesson 22 – Use Sight & Spelling Words

❏ Read the sentences.   ❏ Draw lines to match the words and pictures.

That is actually a very nice head of lettuce.

That member of the staff gave us faithful service!

The small cabin is almost all covered with snow

You can tell he certainly likes being in front of a crowd!

His toy bear is almost as big as he is.

When she was a child, her parents established the fact
that she would practice her music every day.

The medicine bottle is almost full of pills, but
there is a little space at the top.

This member of the police force works in an office.

Two small mice are chewing on some cheese.

Using a motorcycle allows the police officer
to move better in traffic.

There was an emergency, but the ambulance came
and everything is under control.

She has already started filling the cart with groceries,
but there is still some space left.

❏ My student can read and understand these sentences.   Tutor initials _____

Story 22 ◆ King Saul

☐ Read or listen to the story in your native language. I Sam 8:1-9; I Sam 9:1-27; I Sam 10:1-24; I Sam 13:1-14
☐ Find and mark the sight words in the story.   ☐ Listen to the story in English.

actually
almost
already
announced
attack
control
crowd
establish
fact
failed
foolish
forever
head
introduce
kingdom
member
myself
offer
shouted
smallest
supplies
thousand
whose
yourself

The prophet Samuel was the leader of Israel for many years. When he became an old man, the elders of Israel came to him and said, "Before you die, give us a king so we will be like all the other nations around us."

There was a man from the tribe of Benjamin whose name was Saul. He was tall and good looking. In fact, he was head and shoulders taller than almost everyone else.

God told Samuel that Saul would become king. When the prophet told Saul, he answered, "Surely not! I'm from the smallest tribe in Israel. How can this be?"

However, the next morning, Samuel talked to Saul again. The prophet said, "You will be king over the Lord's people."

On a certain day, Samuel called together all the tribes of Israel so he could introduce their new king to them. When the time came, Samuel looked around, but he couldn't see Saul. He prayed and asked God, "Where is he?"

God said, "Look over there. He has hidden himself in the supplies." Some men went and found him and brought him out to stand in front of the crowd.

Samuel announced, "Here is the man the Lord is giving you as king. There isn't anyone like him." The people shouted, "Long live the king!"

The Lord was with Saul and helped him lead the people of Israel. In time, the Philistines came to fight against the Israelites.

King Saul had three thousand men ready for battle against the Philistines. Samuel told Saul to wait for him to come and offer a sacrifice to the Lord before they went into battle. Saul waited seven days, but Samuel didn't come; so he finally offered up the sacrifice himself. Just as he finished, Samuel arrived. He asked, "Saul, what have you done?"

Saul said, "When you didn't come, my men started running away. Actually, most of them are already gone! I was afraid the Philistines would attack, and I needed the Lord's blessing. So, I decided to offer the sacrifice myself."

"You did it yourself? How foolish! You didn't trust the Lord and you didn't obey. This was a test, and you failed it! If you had done right, God would have established your kingdom forever. Now your kingdom will not continue. The Lord is already looking for a man after his own heart. He will become king, and God will establish his kingdom forever."

Saul ruled over Israel for 42 years and did many great things. He led his army well, and they won many battles. However, in King Saul's later years, he wanted to control everyone in his life—even his own family members. King Saul didn't trust in God, and he didn't obey God as he should have.

☐ Read the Story in English.   Tutor initials _____

Review Story 22
Use the words in the boxes to fill in the blanks.

almost crowd fact head introduce smallest supplies whose

1. There was a man from the tribe of Benjamin _____ name was Saul.

2. He was a tall and good looking. In _____, he was _____ and shoulders taller than _____ everyone else.

3. God told Samuel that Saul would become king. When the prophet told Saul, he answered, "Surely not! I'm from the _____ tribe in Israel! How can this be?"

4. On a certain day, Samuel called together all the tribes of Israel so he could _____ their new king to them. Samuel looked around, but he couldn't see Saul because he had hidden himself in the _____. Some men went and found him and brought him out to stand in front of the _____.

Actually already announced attack myself offered shouted thousand

5. Samuel _____, "Here is the man the Lord is giving you as king. There isn't anyone like him." The people _____, "Long live the king!"

6. King Saul had three _____ men ready for battle against the Philistines.

7. Samuel told Saul to wait for him to come and offer a sacrifice to the Lord. Saul waited seven days, but Samuel didn't come; so he finally _____ up the sacrifice himself.

8. Saul said, "When you didn't come, my men started running away. _____, most of them are _____ gone! I was afraid the Philistines would _____, and I needed the Lord's blessing. So I decided to offer the sacrifice _____."

control establish failed foolish forever kingdom members yourself

9. "You did it _____? How _____! You didn't trust the Lord and you didn't obey. This was a test, and you _____ it! If you had done right, God would have established your _____ forever. Now your kingdom will not continue. The Lord is already looking for a man after his own heart. He will become king, and God will _____ his kingdom _____."

10. In King Saul's later years, he wanted to _____ everyone in his life—even his own family _____.

Read the sentences aloud.   Tell the story in your own words.   Tutor initials _____

Vocabulary 22 – What are they thinking or saying?

☐ Read the sentences. ☐ Draw lines to match words and pictures.

I don't have to shout. I can control traffic simply by moving my arms and hands.

I must not fail to practice for my circus act every day.

I've never really thought of myself as beautiful.

I feel established as a member of the staff here. I already have the keys to my new office.

Look, I made it myself!

It is extremely crowded in here! There's not enough space for any more people!

This bowl of rice is all the lunch I need for myself.

Since they are all the same price, I just have to decide which color to buy.

I'm almost dropping something; you could offer to help me!

This math is actually pretty easy, since I've been doing it for so long.

I need to practice my handstand every day.

With these feathers in my head band, I like to think of myself as a chief.

☐ Checked by Tutor   Tutor initials _____

Lesson 23

Phonics Word Reading

Words with "soft g" sound
When the letter g makes the "j" sound – we call it a "soft g"
☐ Practice reading the phonics words until you have mastered them.

Section 1 — words that begin with "soft g"

| gym | ginger | giant | giraffe | gentle | gentleman |
| gem | general | generous | genius | germ | German |

Section 2 — words that contain "soft g"

magic	logic	energy	surgery	allergy	emergency
manage	manager	fragile	religion	engine	engineer
angel	agent	urgent	judgment	danger	dangerous
	apology	imagine	hygiene	vegetables	

Section 3 — words that end with ge

age	cage	page	rage	wage	stage
large	barge	charge	urge	surge	merge
courage	image	college	cottage	garage	rummage
huge	orange	lounge	strange	change	challenge
village	voyage	average	bandage	baggage	cabbage
damage	message	passage	package	language	sausage
mileage	marriage	postage	garbage	storage	advantage

Section 4 — words that end with dge

| ridge | bridge | fridge | grudge | fudge | judge | badge |
| lodge | dodge | edge | hedge | pledge | ledge | knowledge |

☐ My student has mastered the phonics words.   Tutor initials _____

Lesson 23 Spelling (page 1)

Words with "soft g" sound

☐ Read the word list.   ☐ Read each word again and spell it aloud.

age	angel	bridge	charge	college	danger
edge	energy	gentle	giant	gym	judge
knowledge	large	message	package	page	village

☐ Write the word in your language.   ☐ Draw lines to match the words and sentences.
☐ Use the best English word to fill in the blanks.   ☐ Read the sentences aloud.

age _____   They walked across the _____ to get over the little river.
angel _____   At what _____ did the child start school?
bridge _____   When they saw the _____, they were afraid.
charge _____   The fire has been put out, and the family is no longer in _____.
college _____   Their 13-year old daughter was in _____ of the younger children.
danger _____   He attends _____ in the center of the city.

---

edge _____   After a long day, he doesn't have any _____ to play a game.
energy _____   She was afraid when she saw her child at the _____ of the water.
gentle _____   That is truly a _____-size watermelon.
giant _____   Everyone knows that the _____ in that court is fair.
gym _____   I will always remember my _____, white-haired grandmother.
judge _____   He has a certain pair of shoes he always wears in the _____.

---

knowledge _____   She sent us a text _____ saying she will come.
large _____   We can get a _____ number of people in that big bus.
message _____   He has a great deal of _____ about plants.
package _____   That small _____ has only about a hundred people living in it.
page _____   My granddaughter likes to turn each _____ as I read her a story.
village _____   How much will you charge to bring the _____ to my house?

☐ Checked by Tutor   Tutor initials _____

Lesson 23 Spelling (page 2)

Words with "soft g" sound

☐ Read the word list.   ☐ Read each word again and spell it aloud.

| badge | cabbage | orange | giraffe | merge | page |
| bridge | cage | fridge | judge | packages | village |

_____   _____   _____   _____

_____   _____   _____   _____

_____   _____   _____   _____

Spelling Test: ☐ Practice the following words until you have learned them.

1. age
2. angel
3. bridge
4. charge
5. college
6. danger
7. edge
8. energy
9. gentle
10. giant
11. gym
12. judge
13. knowledge
14. large
15. message
16. package
17. page
18. village

☐ My student can spell these words aloud.   Tutor Initials _____

☐ My student can write these words when I read them.   Tutor Initials _____

Lesson 23 Sight Words

☐ Write the word in your language.
☐ Practice reading the words until you can pronounce them correctly.

agree	ahead	along
bear	began	daily
does	experience	forward
held	officer	possible
receive	sight	sling
smooth	stood	stream
successful	toward	upon
valley	within	worry

☐ My student can read these words and knows their meanings.   Tutor Initials _____

Lesson 23 – Use Sight & Spelling Words

☐ Read the sentences.   ☐ Draw lines to match the words and pictures.

It is not possible to get a car in that garage because it is full of junk.

When it began to rain, he still stood there looking at things in the yard sale.

We walked along the stream and saw a gorge with a tree making a bridge between the two sides.

It doesn't seem possible that he could be successful and win a fight with that lion.

We need to plan ahead because our fuel gauge shows we are moving toward empty.

David had years of experience using smooth stones in a sling something like this.

As soon as we came within sight, the little dog stood up with its paws on the edge of the box.

I received a small package, but I didn't know ahead of time what a special gift it held!

We suddenly saw a giant leopard coming toward us, slowly moving along the edge of the ledge.

He looked back, and now he's in danger of falling forward.

There's a message on the table within sight of anyone who comes into the room.

Some people would gladly agree to put all these vegetables into a blender and make a "smoothie" for their daily energy drink.

☐ My student can read and understand these sentences.   Tutor initials _____

Story 23 ◆ David as a Young Man

☐ Read or listen to the story in your native language. I Sam 16:1-13; I Sam 17:1-58
☐ Find and mark the sight words in the story. ☐ Listen to the story in English.

agreed
ahead
along
bear
began
daily
does
experience
forward
held
officer
possible
receive
sight
sling
smooth
stood
stream
successful
toward
upon
valley
within
worry

God told the prophet Samuel to go to Bethlehem and anoint one of Jesse's sons to be the next king of Israel. God told Samuel ahead of time, "Don't look on the outside—how tall a man is or how strong. I see things you can't see. I look on the heart."

As Jesse brought out each of his sons to meet the prophet, Samuel said, "He's not the one." Finally he asked, "Don't you have any other children?"

"Only one more—David, my youngest. He's out watching the sheep."

"Send for him!" As soon as David walked into the room, the Lord said, "This is the one!" So, Samuel anointed David with oil, and the Spirit of God came upon him. He kept taking care of his father's sheep, but the power of God was with him.

At that time, the Philistines brought their army into Israel. They set up camp on one hill, and the Israelites set up camp on another hill, with a valley between them.

One of the Philistine soldiers was a man named Goliath. He was 9 feet, 9 inches tall. Every day, Goliath would come out and dare someone to fight him, but the Israelite soldiers just stood there in fear! Goliath would say, "If your man kills me, then we will be your slaves. But, if I kill your man, you will be our slaves."

King Saul announced that if any person could kill the giant, he would receive many gifts, and he would also receive the king's daughter as his wife.

During that time, David's father sent him to visit his brothers in the army. He said, "Bring me back word on how the battle is going." When David arrived, Goliath began his daily shouting.

David asked, "Who does this Philistine think he is? He insults the army of the living God!"

Someone told King Saul what David was saying, and the king sent for him. David said, "Don't worry about this Philistine. I'll fight him."

The king said, "You can't fight him! He is strong and has years of experience. It's not possible for you to win over him."

David answered, "Oh, yes it is! When I was watching my father's sheep, sometimes a lion or a bear would come and take one of my lambs. I have killed both a lion and a bear, and I'll do the same thing to Goliath. The Lord will give him to me." King Saul finally agreed.

David went down along a stream and found five smooth stones to use in his sling. Then he moved toward the giant. As soon as David was within sight of him, Goliath began shouting, "Am I a dog that you come against me with sticks? I will feed you to the birds!"

David shouted back, "You come to me with a sword and a spear, but I come to you in the name of the Lord!" Then David ran toward the giant. He put a stone in his sling and shot Goliath in the middle of his forehead. The giant fell forward and hit the ground, face down. David ran and pulled out Goliath's sword and killed him. He cut off his head and held it up for all to see. Then David took the head of Goliath and went in to see the king.

King Saul made David an officer in the army, and David was successful in everything Saul told him to do. Many years later, Saul and his sons were all killed in battle. Then the people came and made David their king.

☐ Read the Story in English.   Tutor initials _____

Review Story 23

Use the words in the boxes to fill in the blanks.

| ahead | daily | does | receive | stood | upon | valley |

1. God told Samuel _____ of time, "Don't look on the outside — how tall a man is or how strong. I see things you can't see. I look on the heart."

2. Samuel anointed David with oil, and the Spirit of God came _____ him.

3. The Philistines set up camp on one hill, and the Israelites set up camp on another hill, with a _____ between them.

4. Every day, Goliath would come out and dare someone to fight him, but the Israelite soldiers just _____ there in fear!

5. King Saul announced that if any person could kill the giant, he would _____ many gifts, and he would also receive the king's daughter as his wife.

6. David's father sent him to visit his brothers in the army. When David arrived, Goliath began his _____ shouting. David asked, "Who _____ this Philistine think he is?"

| agreed | along | bear | experience | possible | sling | smooth | stream | worry |

7. Someone told King Saul what David was saying, and the king sent for him. David said, "Don't _____ about this Philistine. I'll fight him."

8. The king said, "You can't fight him! He is strong and has years of _____. It's not _____ for you to win over him."

9. David answered, "Oh, yes, it is! When I was watching my father's sheep, sometimes a lion or a _____ would come and take one of my lambs. I have killed both a lion and a bear, and I'll do the same thing to Goliath." King Saul finally _____.

10. David went down _____ a _____ and found five _____ stones to use in his _____.

| began | forward | held | officer | sight | successful | toward | within |

11. As soon as David was _____ _____ of him, Goliath _____ shouting, "Am I a dog that you come against me with sticks? I will feed you to the birds!"

12. David ran _____ the giant. He put a stone in his sling and shot Goliath in the middle of his forehead. The giant fell _____ and hit the ground, face down. David ran and pulled out Goliath's sword and killed him. He cut off his head and _____ it up for all to see.

13. King Saul made David an _____ in the army, and David was _____ in everything Saul told him to do.

Read the sentences aloud.   Tell the story in your own words.   Tutor initials _____

Vocabulary 23 ~ What are they thinking or saying?

☐ Read the sentences.   ☐ Draw lines to match words and pictures.

We've had a successful meeting. I'm glad we could agree on a plan for moving forward.

Now that I have my hat and my badge, everyone in the village will know that I'm the officer in charge.

I like sitting on this ledge eating my sandwich.

Speaking from my knowledge and experience, I don't think it's possible to fix this TV.

I wear a mask and gloves to protect both myself and you from any possible germs that could be a danger to us.

Wow! That is such a large bandage! Does it have to be changed daily?

This is a huge energy bill! There must have been a large number of hidden charges.

I will soon have this engine running smoothly.

My daily job is to trim the hedges. I manage my own time, and no one else has to worry about it.

My dark sunglasses help me see any danger ahead.

Why are these things here? We agreed ahead of time there would be no baggage along the edge of the dock.

I have a lot of knowledge and experience. If you will receive my advice, you will be successful.

☐ Checked by Tutor   Tutor initials _____

Lesson 24

Phonics Word Reading

"r-controlled vowels" ~ Words with er ir ur ear ere

☐ Practice reading the phonics words until you have mastered them.

Section 1 ~ words containing er

her	herd	germ	clerk	person	perfect	percent
merge	mercy	serve	server	servant	service	deserve
enter	water	better	never	ever	every	very
after	anger	cover	finger	tender	member	leader
offer	letter	summer	winter	river	matter	answer
later	maker	chapter	brother	sister	teacher	shepherd

Section 2 ~ words containing ir

sir	stir	firm	first	third	thirst	thirsty
girl	dirt	dirty	chirp	bird	birth	birthday
circle	circus	giraffe	mirror	shirt	skirt	squirrel

Section 3 ~ words containing ur

fur	purr	spur	urge	urgent	burst	burrito
churn	burn	burned	hurt	turn	return	during
curl	curb	disturb	jury	hurry	surf	surface
murder	nurse	curse	cursed	purse	church	surge
surprise	turkey	turtle	purple	furnace	purpose	Thursday

Section 4 ~ words containing ear & ere

| earth | early | earn | learn | heard | pearl | were |

☐ My student has mastered the phonics words.   Tutor initials _____

Lesson 24 Spelling (page 1)

The /er/ sound spelled with er ir ur ear ere

☐ Read the word list.   ☐ Read each word again and spell it aloud.

after	better	birth	cover	early	earth
ever	girl	heard	hurry	hurt	learn
never	person	third	turn	very	water

☐ Write the word in your language.   ☐ Draw lines to match the words and sentences.
☐ Use the best English word to fill in the blanks.   ☐ Read the sentences aloud.

after _____   I feel _____ today than I did yesterday.

better _____   The _____ of my workbook is green.

birth _____   The baby will go to sleep soon _____ supper.

cover _____   A large part of the _____ is covered by water.

early _____   Our teacher always comes _____ to class.

earth _____   After the _____ of their child, they moved to a larger apartment.

ever _____   Let's walk slowly; there's no reason to _____ today.

girl _____   She is the only _____ in her family; all the other children are boys.

heard _____   Have you _____ been to a circus?

hurry _____   He really wants to _____ English!

hurt _____   I have not _____ anything about a party on Friday.

learn _____   If your shoes are too small, they can _____ your feet.

never _____   There is room for one more _____ in this car.

person _____   She has _____ been out of the country where she was born.

third _____   I like these yams; in fact, I like them _____ much.

turn _____   This is the _____ time she has lost her glasses.

very _____   May I have a drink of _____?

water _____   We need to _____ left at the next road.

☐ Checked by Tutor   Tutor initials _____

Lesson 24 Spelling (page 2)

Words spelled with er ir ur ear ere

Read all the words.   Write the best word under each picture.

| turkey | girl | turtle | skirt | surprised | turn |
| fern | nurse | purse | squirrel | third | bird |

_____   _____   _____   _____

_____   _____   _____   _____

_____   _____   _____   _____

Spelling Test: Practice the following words until you have learned them.

1. after
2. better
3. birth
4. cover
5. early
6. earth
7. ever
8. girl
9. heard
10. hurry
11. hurt
12. learn
13. never
14. person
15. third
16. turn
17. very
18. water

My student can spell these words aloud.   Tutor Initials _____

My student can write these words when I read them.   Tutor Initials _____

Lesson 24 Sight Words

☐ Write the word in your language.
☐ Practice reading the words until you can pronounce them correctly.

afterward	alone	commander
cruel	defend	deserve
expect	forgive	given
instead	invite	judge
known	letter	openly
says	secret	situation
slept	solution	surprise
usually	worst	wrote

☐ My student can read these words and knows their meanings. Tutor Initials _____

Lesson 24 – Use Sight & Spelling Words

☐ Read the sentences.   ☐ Draw lines to match the words and pictures.

Our first aid kit is a box with a handle on the cover, two latches, and a cross on the front.

It is perched on a branch, chirping loudly, with its mouth wide open.

If there's not a person at the desk, ring that bell, and usually someone comes quickly.

She sits alone on a bench in early fall.

He slept in a tent last night, and now he is stirring his food in a pot over an open fire.

He is in a hurry to open the gift. What's inside will not be a secret much longer.

He usually checks his shirt and tie in a mirror before getting up to speak.

He learned as a young child, and now it seems like he's always known how to milk a cow.

He came very early, but he is still waiting for his turn to see the nurse.

I was surprised to find out there is no meat in that burger. It is actually a "veggie burger."

He will hurry and put him to bed, expecting that he'll sleep until morning.

She never wants her picture taken, so she turns her head.

☐ My student can read and understand these sentences.   Tutor initials _____

Story 24 ◆ David as King

☐ Read or listen to the story in your native language. II Sam 5:1-4; II Sam 11:1-27; II Sam 12:1-25
☐ Find and mark the sight words in the story.   ☐ Listen to the story in English.

afterward
alone
commander
cruel
defended
deserves
expecting
forgive
given
instead
invited
judge
known
letter
openly
says
secret
situation
slept
solution
surprised
usually
worst
wrote

David established his kingdom and defended it from the nations around him. His fame spread everywhere. He became known as the greatest king of Israel.

King David usually went with his army into battle. But one time, he decided to stay home. In the evening, he went out on the roof of his palace. From there, he saw a beautiful woman taking a bath. He found out she was Bathsheba, the wife of one of his best soldiers who was away in the army.

David had Bathsheba brought to his palace, and they slept together. Not long after, she sent word to the king, "I'm expecting a baby." In order to hide what he had done, David ordered her husband, Uriah, to come home. When he arrived, they talked about the war. Then David told him to go home to his wife.

Uriah left, but he didn't go home. Instead, he slept at the door of the palace. In the morning, David was surprised. He asked Uriah, "Why didn't you go home?"

Uriah answered, "The army of Israel is outside sleeping in tents. I can't go to my house and be with my wife while my men are on the battlefield!"

That evening, David invited Uriah to eat with him. They ate and drank until the soldier was drunk, but he still didn't go home to his wife.

David knew he was in a bad situation! He needed to find a solution for this problem. He wrote a letter to the army commander, and sent it back to the battlefield with Uriah. The letter said, "Put Uriah in the front lines where the fighting is the worst. At a certain time, tell all the men to pull back except Uriah, leaving him alone to be killed."

So Uriah died in battle. Then David brought Bathsheba to the palace to be his wife. Soon afterward, she gave birth to a son.

The Lord sent a prophet, Nathan, with a message for David: "Two men lived in the same city. One was rich and had a large flock of sheep. The other was poor and had only one small lamb – a pet that was like a child to him. One day, the rich man had someone come to eat with him. He didn't want to kill one of his own sheep and serve it for a meal. Instead, he stole the poor man's little lamb, killed it, and ate it."

David was angry! He shouted, "How dare that man! How could he be so cruel? He deserves to die. He will pay four times over for what he has done!"

Nathan pointed at David and said, "You are the man! The Lord says, 'I made you king over Israel, and I gave you all you have. If you had asked, I would have given you more. So why have you done this evil? You killed Uriah and took his wife. You did all this in secret, but I will judge you openly.' "

David said, "I have sinned against the Lord." Then he begged God to forgive him.

The prophet Nathan said, "The Lord has heard your prayer and has taken away your sin. You won't die, but the baby will." So the first child of David and Bathsheba died. Later, they had another son and named him Solomon. The Lord promised that Solomon would be the next king of Israel.

☐ Read the Story in English.   Tutor initials _____

Review Story 24

Use the words in the boxes to fill in the blanks.

| defended   expecting   Instead   invited   known   slept   surprised   usually |

1. David established his kingdom and _____ it from the nations around him. His fame spread everywhere. He became _____ as the greatest king of Israel.
2. King David _____ went with his army into battle. But one time, he decided to stay home. In the evening, he went out on the roof of his palace. From there he saw a beautiful woman taking a bath.
3. David had Bathsheba brought to his palace and they _____ together. Not long after, she sent word to the king, "I'm _____ a baby." In order to hide what he had done, David ordered her husband, Uriah, to come home. When he arrived, they talked about the war. Then David told him to go home to his wife.
4. Uriah left, but he didn't go home. _____, he slept at the door of the palace.
5. In the morning, David was _____. He asked Uriah, "Why didn't you go home?"
6. That evening, David _____ Uriah to eat with him. They ate and drank, until the soldier was drunk, but he still didn't go home to his wife.

| afterward   alone   commander   letter   situation   solution   worst   wrote |

7. David knew he was in a bad _____! He needed to find a _____ for this problem. He _____ a letter to the army _____.
8. The _____ said, "Put Uriah in the front lines where the fighting is the _____. At a certain time, tell all the men to pull back except Uriah, leaving him _____ to be killed."
9. So, Uriah died in battle. Then David brought Bathsheba to the palace to be his wife. Soon _____ she gave birth to a son.

| cruel   deserves   forgive   given   judge   openly   says   secret |

10. The Lord sent a prophet, Nathan, with a message for David. He told about a rich man who stole a poor man's little pet lamb, killed it, and ate it. David was angry! He shouted, "How dare that man! How could he be so _____? He _____ to die!"
11. Nathan pointed at David and said, "You are the man! The Lord _____, 'I made you king over Israel, and I gave you all you have. If you had asked, I would have _____ you more. So why have you done this evil? You killed Uriah and took his wife. You did all this in _____, but I will _____ you _____.' "
12. David said, "I have sinned against the Lord." Then he begged God to _____ him.

Read the sentences aloud.   Tell the story in your own words.   Tutor initials _____

Vocabulary 24 – What are they thinking or saying?

☐ Read the sentences. ☐ Draw lines to match words and pictures.

It's my turn to serve the soup, and I'm getting better at it all the time!

The boss wrote you a secret message. You'd better hurry and read it.

My nurse says the worst is over; but I still hurt all over. At least my feet are warm.

Surprise! Happy Birthday!

There is only one solution. I expect you to go in there alone and ask him to forgive you.

I feel so alone. I keep expecting maybe someone will invite me to join in their game.

I usually don't have this much trouble thinking of a solution, but this is the worst possible situation!

You surprised me. I didn't expect to see you here!

I hope she likes what I wrote. It says she is a very nice person and I've learned so much from her.

No one knows the way I make this. I never wrote it down, and I've never given the secret to anyone.

First, let me say, you deserve to know the true situation with your car. It will be better if you're not surprised after we fix it.

I never want to be cruel or hurt this fish. I'd better hurry and get it back into the water.

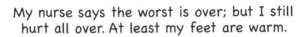

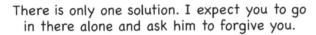

☐ Checked by Tutor   Tutor initials _____

Lesson 25

Phonics Word Reading

"r-controlled vowels" — Words with ar, or, our

☐ Practice reading the phonics words until you have mastered them.

Section 1 — words containing ar

bar	far	jar	car	card	tar	target
barber	barn	harp	yard	hard	hardware	harvest
are	arch	march	harsh	barge	large	charge
arm	army	harm	farm	charm	alarm	argue
ark	mark	bark	dark	shark	sharp	heart
star	start	part	apart	party	pardon	garden
art	cart	smart	chart	park	spark	market

Section 2 — words containing or

order	for	fork	fort	form	uniform	force
forward	poor	door	floor	north	normal	score
born	corn	horn	worn	torn	thorn	morning
sort	sport	port	passport	support	report	record
pork	porch	torch	short	more	core	correct
sore	wore	tore	dorm	storm	store	story
before	effort	glory	honor	tractor	harbor	alligator
horse	sword	motor	razor	labor	favor	favorite
color	pastor	doctor	actor	author	tutor	mentor
creator	sailor	mayor	major	visitor	victor	victory

Section 3 — Words with -ar- sounding like "or"

war   wart   award   reward   toward   warm   warn   warning

Section 4 — Words with -our sounding like "or"

court   course   mourn   your   pour   four   fourth

Section 5 — Words with -or- sounding like "er"

word   work   worm   world   worry   worst   worship

☐ My student has mastered the phonics words.   Tutor initials _____

Lesson 25 Spelling (page 1)

"r-controlled vowels" ~ Words with ar, or, our

☐ Read the word list.   ☐ Read each word again and spell it aloud.

before	door	far	for	force	four
hard	mark	more	order	part	poor
short	start	word	work	world	your

☐ Write the word in your language.   ☐ Draw lines to match the words and sentences.
☐ Use the best English word to fill in the blanks.   ☐ Read the sentences aloud.

before _____   How _____ did they travel today?

door _____   He likes to walk outside _____ breakfast.

far _____   I have a gift _____ my teacher.

for _____   She has _____ young children—two girls and two boys.

force _____   If you open the _____, you will be surprised.

four _____   The lid is nailed shut, but you can _____ it open.

---

hard _____   She doesn't know that there's a _____ on the back of her shirt.

mark _____   My boss is glad he has _____ workers now than he did last year.

more _____   He has a _____ bed; it's just a mat on the floor.

order _____   He grew up in a _____ family, but now he owns his own shop.

part _____   I like the first _____ of the story, but it has a sad ending.

poor _____   When the commander gives an _____, all the men obey.

---

short _____   They will _____ on their journey early tomorrow morning.

start _____   We must hurry because it's only a _____ time before sunset.

word _____   You need to wash _____ hands before preparing our food.

world _____   He was suddenly called into _____ late this evening.

work _____   That ship has been all the way around the _____.

your _____   I don't understand, because I don't know the meaning of that _____.

☐ Checked by Tutor   Tutor initials _____

Lesson 25 Spelling (page 2)

"r-controlled vowels" – Words with ar, or, our

☐ Read all the words.   ☐ Write the best word under each picture.

| barn | cart | corn | fork | horn | storyteller |
| torch | chart | door | four | horse | carpenter |

_____   _____   _____   _____   _____

_____   _____   _____   _____

   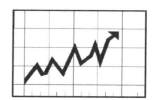   

_____   _____   _____   _____

Spelling Test: ☐ Practice the following words until you have learned them.

1. before
2. door
3. far
4. for
5. force
6. four
7. hard
8. mark
9. more
10. order
11. part
12. poor
13. short
14. start
15. word
16. work
17. world
18. your

☐ My student can spell these words aloud.   Tutor Initials _____

☐ My student can write these words when I read them.   Tutor Initials _____

Lesson 25 Sight Words

☐ Write the word in your language.
☐ Practice reading the words until you can pronounce them correctly.

addition	appear	area
argument	beside	complete
divide	example	follow
half	increase	learn
location	material	matter
method	often	organize
realize	simple	understand
valuable	wealth	wisdom

☐ My student can read these words and knows their meanings.   Tutor Initials _____

Lesson 25 – Use Sight & Spelling Words

☐ Read the sentences.   ☐ Draw lines to match the words and pictures.

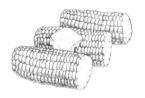

She sits beside him and helps him
understand the hard parts of the story.

The fort is in a good location, far above sea level,
on the top part of the hill.

The bread has been divided into two parts.

Her clothes and boots are
made with valuable materials.

The child is still learning to walk.

At work, he points to marks on a chart
to show the increase in sales.

The method we use in order to make more servings
is to cut the ears of corn in half before cooking.

One method for catching fish is
with a worm on a hook.

The old brick barn has three doors
that are arch shaped.

She keeps her hair completely covered
while working in her yard or garden.

He pours carefully because
he wants the cup just half full.

That bookmark is made of beautiful silk material.
It shows us where to start reading again.

☐ My student can read and understand these sentences.   Tutor initials _____

Story 25 ◆ King Solomon

☐ Read or listen to the story in your native language. I Kings 3:1-28; I Kings 6:1-13; I Kings 9:1-9
☐ Find and mark the sight words in the story.   ☐ Listen to the story in English.

addition
appeared
area
argument
beside
complete
divide
example
follow
half
increased
learn
location
material
matter
method
often
organized
realized
simple
understand
valuable
wealth
wisdom

After David died, Solomon became king of Israel. He loved the Lord and tried to follow the example of his father. One night, the Lord appeared to him in a dream and asked, "What do you want me to give you?"

Solomon answered, "My father was a great king, but I feel like a child who doesn't know anything. Please give me understanding to rule your people wisely."

The Lord said, "You have asked for wisdom instead of long life, riches, or peace. Therefore, I will give you wisdom. In addition, I will give you riches and honor. If you continue to follow me like your father did, I will also give you a long life."

Soon afterward, two women came to Solomon and asked him to settle an argument. One of them was holding a baby. The first one said, "This woman and I live in the same house. I gave birth to a son, and three days later she gave birth to a son. One night, while we were sleeping, her baby died. So she took my living baby and then put her dead son beside me. When I woke up in the morning, I realized what had happened. The dead child was not my son, but hers. She has my baby!"

The other woman said, "No, the living child is mine and the dead one is hers." Solomon called one of his guards, "Come here with a sword." Pointing to the baby, he said, "Divide the child in two and give each mother a half."

One woman cried out, "No, don't kill my son! She can have him. Let him live!"

The other woman said, "Yes, cut the child in half, so we will both have a part."

The king turned to the guard, "This is a simple matter. Give the baby to the first woman. I know she is the real mother because she truly loves the child."

When the people of Israel heard this true story, they knew that God had given great wisdom to Solomon. God also gave him much wealth.

The king knew it was God's plan for him to build the House of the Lord, the Temple. Solomon organized a workforce of skilled craftsmen. They used many valuable materials to build the Temple—huge rocks, cedar trees, gold, silver, and brass. Solomon didn't want the sound of tools at the location, so they used a special method. Rocks and trees were cut to size before they were brought to the Temple site. It took seven years to complete the job.

God spoke to Solomon again, "If you continue to obey me as your father did, I will establish your kingdom forever. But if you or your sons turn away from me, I will take Israel off this land, and the Temple will be destroyed."

Over the 40 years that Solomon ruled Israel, he increased in both wisdom and riches. His fame spread to the area all around Israel. People often came from other countries to learn from him and to see his great wealth. The people lived in peace all the years that Solomon was king.

☐ Read the Story in English.   Tutor initials _____

Review Story 25
Use the words in the boxes to fill in the blanks.

| addition | appeared | example | follow | understanding | wisdom |

1. Solomon loved the Lord and tried to follow the _____ of his father.
2. The Lord _____ to him and asked, "What do you want me to give you?"
3. "Please give me _____ to rule your people wisely."
4. The Lord said, "You have asked for _____ instead of long life, riches, or peace. Therefore, I will give you wisdom. In _____, I will give you riches and honor. If you continue to _____ me like your father did, I will also give you a long life."

| argument | beside | Divide | half | matter | realized | simple | wealth |

5. Soon afterward, two women came to Solomon and asked him to settle an _____.
6. While they were sleeping, one of their babies died. The mother of the dead child took the living baby from the other woman and put the dead one _____ her.
7. When they woke up in the morning, the other woman _____ what had happened.
8. The king called one of his guards, "Come here with a sword. Pointing to the baby, he said, "_____ the child in two and give each mother a half." One woman cried out, "No, don't kill my son! She can have him. Let him live!"
9. The other woman said, "Yes, cut the child in _____, so we will both have a part."
10. The king turned to the guard, "This is a _____ _____. Give the baby to the first woman. I know she is the real mother because she truly loves the child."
11. God had given great wisdom to Solomon. God also gave him much _____.

| area | complete | increased | learn | location | materials | method | often | organized | valuable |

12. Solomon _____ a workforce of skilled craftsmen.
13. They used many _____ _____ to build the Temple.
14. Solomon didn't want the sound of tools at the _____, so they used a special _____. It took seven years to _____ the job.
15. Over the 40 years that Solomon ruled Israel, he _____ in both wisdom and riches. His fame spread to the _____ all around Israel.
16. People _____ came from other countries to _____ from him and to see his great wealth.

Read the sentences aloud.   Tell the story in your own words.   Tutor initials _____

Vocabulary 25 ~ What are they thinking or saying?

❏ Read the sentences. ❏ Draw lines to match words and pictures.

It never really gets warm
in the part of the world where I live.

I'm so happy.
I get to start my new job next week!

Here is the only part I don't understand.

I can hardly believe I'm fourteen already!

I need to organize my thoughts
before I start writing anything.

I'm looking for a certain location, but
I don't understand this map

This sharpener does not work right.
It's using up half my pencil!

I learned how to fix this problem long ago.
It will be simple!

I don't understand how this insect could appear
in this part of the world.

I want to get my jacket completely on
before I go out the door.

I'm not sure what to think about this report.

I don't want to stay in there, and I
have learned how to get out.

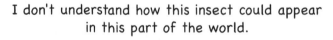

❏ Checked by Tutor   Tutor initials _____

Lesson 26

Phonics Word Reading

The /ou/ sound spelled with ou & ow

☐ Practice reading the phonics words until you have mastered them.

Section 1 — Making the /ou/ sound with ou

out	pout	shout	scout	about	without
round	around	ground	mound	found	founder
sound	hound	pound	bound	abound	surround
south	mouth	proud	cloud	loud	aloud
count	account	mount	amount	mountain	thousand
mouse	house	couch	bounce	ounce	announce
our	sour	flour	hour	foul	lounge

Section 2 — Making the /ou/ sound with ow

now	bow	brow	brown	frown	down
vow	vowel	towel	plow	town	gown
how	however	howl	owl	growl	scowl
meow	allow	allowed	drown	drowned	drowsy
cow	cowboy	crown	crowd	chow	chowder
shower	flower	power	powder	tower	watchtower

Section 3 — More words with ou & ow

outer   workout   cookout   downstairs   downward   downhill

birdhouse   doghouse   hothouse   farmhouse   firehouse   warehouse

☐ My student has mastered the phonics words.   Tutor initials _____

Lesson 26 Spelling (page 1)
The /ou/ sound spelled with ou & ow

☐ Read the word list.   ☐ Read each word again and spell it aloud.

about	amount	around	brown	down	found
ground	hour	house	how	loud	now
our	out	power	shout	sound	town

☐ Write the word in your language.   ☐ Draw lines to match the words and sentences.
☐ Use the best English word to fill in the blanks.   ☐ Read the sentences aloud.

about _____   She likes to put a large _____ of butter on her bread.
amount _____   It's possible to walk _____ that lake in less than an hour.
around _____   I like learning _____ the moon and stars.
brown _____   The old man lost his glasses again, but we _____ them for him.
down _____   I don't like to see the leaves of that plant turn _____.
found _____   Someone will go _____ under the street to fix that pipe.

our _____   She says she would be completely happy to live in a small _____.
hour _____   If you show me _____ to change the tire, I can do it.
house _____   Their lunch _____ is from 12 noon until one o'clock.
how _____   My grandmother says the music is too _____.
loud _____   I like to hear the _____ of children playing quietly.
sound _____   My grandfather is the best storyteller in _____ family.

ground _____   When she heard the loud sound, she came _____ to see what happened
out _____   I can't talk _____, but we can visit after I finish work.
power _____   Those kids think it's fun to sit on the _____ and eat lunch.
shout _____   They live in a small _____ where almost everyone knows each other
now _____   He doesn't have the _____ to get the young man out of prison.
town _____   Please don't _____ at the children; talk quietly.

☐ Checked by Tutor   Tutor initials _____

Lesson 26 Spelling (page 2)

The /ou/ sound may be spelled ou & ow

☐ Read all the words.   ☐ Write the best word under each picture.

| bow | clown | crown | mouse | tower | dog house |
| clouds | cow | flowers | owl | town | paper towels |

Spelling Test: ☐ Practice the following words until you have learned them.

1. about	4. brown	7. ground	10. how	13. our	16. shout
2. amount	5. down	8. hour	11. loud	14. out	17. sound
3. around	6. found	9. house	12. now	15. power	18. town

☐ My student can spell these words aloud.   Tutor Initials _____

☐ My student can write these words when I read them.   Tutor Initials _____

Lesson 26 Sight Words

☐ Write the word in your language.
☐ Practice reading the words until you can pronounce them correctly.

accept	anything	anywhere
body	capture	careful
carry	certainly	climb
couple	difficult	disease
easy	heavy	kneel
longer	possibly	refuse
return	school	student
terrible	visitor	white

☐ My student can read these words and knows their meanings.   Tutor Initials _____

Lesson 26 – Use Sight & Spelling Words

☐ Read the sentences.   ☐ Draw lines to match the words and pictures.

The servants are carefully carrying
a heavy water jug.

It is easy for the kids to climb up into their tree
house and climb back down to the ground.

If you listen, you can hear the loud sound of
a wolf howling at the moon.

The flower girl will walk carefully and carry
the basket down to the front of the church.

It's just after the midnight hour, and this
couple is having a difficult time
trying to stop the loud crying of their baby.

How nice! This happy couple has just now
gotten married. She has a white dress
and he has a brown suit.

When he prays, he kneels down on the ground.

If you climb up into the carriage and
pay the driver the right amount of money,
you can go anywhere in town.

The mother is carrying her baby in her pouch.

Our dog has been trained to carry something in its
mouth anywhere we tell him to take it.

Our adult students are allowed to have drinks
anywhere in the building, if they are careful.

That animal was captured in Africa
and now lives in a zoo in our town.

☐ My student can read and understand these sentences.   Tutor initials _____

Story 26 ◆ Naaman

☐ Read or listen to the story in your native language. II Kings 5:1-27
☐ Find and mark the sight words in the story.   ☐ Listen to the story in English.

accept
anything
anywhere
body
capture
carefully
carry
certainly
climb
couple
difficult
disease
easy
heavy
kneel
longer
possibly
refused
return
school
student
terrible
visitors
white

Naaman was a successful commander in the Syrian army, but he had leprosy, a terrible disease of the skin. During a war with Israel, he captured a young girl and brought her home to be a servant for his wife. The girl said, "I wish my master could go to Israel. Our prophet, Elisha, can heal people with leprosy." Someone told Naaman what the girl had said. So Naaman and his men prepared their horses, chariots, money, and gifts. They went to Israel to see the prophet.

When they arrived at the house of the prophet, Elisha sent his servant out to tell Naaman what to do. "Go wash in the Jordan River, here in Israel. Dip down into it seven times, and you will be healed."

Naaman was angry! He said, "I thought surely the prophet would come out, stand in front of me, pray to the Lord, wave his hand over my body, and heal me. If I'm going to wash in a river, I'll go to one of the beautiful rivers of Syria, not a muddy river like the Jordan." So he turned and went away in a rage.

Naaman's men spoke very carefully to him. "If the prophet had asked you to do something difficult, you would have done it. But he told you to do something easy—wash and be clean." So Naaman decided to obey the prophet. He went to the Jordan River and dipped down into it seven times. Suddenly his skin was healed just as the prophet said it would be! In fact, it was like the skin of a young boy.

After Naaman was healed, he and his men went back to the prophet's house. "Now I know that there is no god on the earth except the God of Israel. Please accept the gifts I brought for you."

Elisha refused, "No, I will not accept a gift from you."

Naaman said, "Then please give me as much soil as two mules can haul. I will no longer worship any other god. When I kneel and worship the Lord God, I will have this soil from Israel."

After Naaman and his men left to return home, Elisha's servant decided to go and ask for a gift. So he ran after the chariot. When Naaman saw him coming, he stopped the chariot, climbed down, and asked, "Is everything all right?"

"Everything is fine. My master just found out he has visitors coming tonight. They are students from the School of the Prophets. Can you possibly give us some things for them—a couple changes of clothes and some silver?"

"Certainly! Here are some nice clothes and 150 pounds of silver." Naaman then had his men carry the heavy load back to the servant's house.

When the servant came back, Elisha asked, "Where did you go?"

He answered, "I didn't go anywhere."

Elisha said, "Didn't my spirit go with you? It was not right for you to accept anything from Naaman. Now his leprosy will come upon you." The servant looked down at his arms, and they were already turning white with leprosy!

☐ Read the Story in English.   Tutor initials _____

Review Story 26

Use the words in the boxes to fill in the blanks.

| body | captured | carefully | difficult | disease | easy | terrible |

1. Naaman was a successful commander in the Syrian army, but he had leprosy, a _____ _____ of the skin.
2. During a war with Israel, he _____ a young girl and brought her home to be a servant for his wife. The girl told about a prophet who could heal people with leprosy.
3. When Naaman and his men arrived at the house of the prophet, Elisha sent his servant to tell him what to do. Naaman was angry! He said, "I thought surely the prophet would come out, stand in front of me, pray to the Lord, wave his hand over my _____, and heal me."
4. Naaman's men spoke very _____ to him. "If the prophet had asked you to do something _____, you would have done it. But he told you to do something _____."

| accept | climbed | kneel | longer | refused | return | School | students | visitors |

5. After Naaman was healed, he and his men went back to the prophet's house. He said, "Please _____ the gifts I brought for you." Elisha _____.
6. Naaman said, "Then please give me as much soil as two mules can haul. I will no _____ worship any other god. When I _____ and worship the Lord God, I will have this soil from Israel."
7. After Naaman left to _____ home, Elisha's servant decided to go and ask for a gift.
8. Naaman stopped the chariot, _____ down and asked, "Is everything all right?"
9. The servant said, "My master just found out he has _____ coming tonight.
10. They are _____ from the _____ of the Prophets."

| anything | anywhere | carry | Certainly | couple | heavy | possibly | white |

11. Can you _____ give us some things for them – a _____ changes of clothes and some silver?"
12. "_____! Here are some nice clothes and 150 pounds of silver." Naaman then had his men _____ the _____ load back to the servant's house.
13. Elisha asked, "Where did you go?" His servant answered, "I didn't go _____."
14. Elisha said, "It was not right for you to accept _____ from Naaman. Now his leprosy will come upon you."
15. The servant looked down at his arms. They were already turning _____ with leprosy!

Read the sentences aloud.   Tell the story in your own words.   Tutor initials _____

Vocabulary 26 ~ What are they thinking or saying?

☐ Read the sentences.   ☐ Draw lines to match words and pictures.

We always show our visitors around the grounds.
We are proud of what our workmen have built here.

It will not be difficult for the crowd to hear me.
I won't have to shout.

I feel like I'm about to drop something.

The sound of that loud noise is terrible!
Is there anything you can do about it?

This little boat seems almost too small for my body,
but if I'm careful and don't move much, I think
I can make it across the river.

I feel so happy and proud.
I wasn't expecting anything!

For me this is easy. I move my body to
keep the hoops going around me.

Don't worry. I won't try to climb down
from this chair. It's about time to eat!

I like how she always says,
"If you need anything, let me know."

I can't possibly work any longer.
I have a terrible headache!

It's easy to take a heavy load almost anywhere
when I carry it this way.

It is certainly going to take a huge
amount of paint for that bell tower.

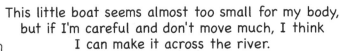
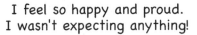

☐ Checked by Tutor   Tutor initials _____

Lesson 27
Phonics Word Reading
Special Spellings and Silent Letters

☐ Practice reading the phonics words until you have mastered them.

Section 1 — Irregular Spellings

are   was   says   said   again   women   busy   business   minute
people   sure   sugar   bear   wear   pear   bury   marry   carry   choir

Section 2 — gh sounds like f

laugh   enough   rough   tough   cough

Section 3 — ph sounds like f

phone   microphone   headphones   photo   phonics   alphabet   elephant   prophet

Section 4 — Silent l

talk   walk   half   calf   would   could   should

Section 5 — Silent k

knife   knock   knob   knee   kneel   knew   know   known

Section 6 — Silent b

lamb   limb   climb   comb   tomb   thumb   plumber   doubt

Section 7 — Silent u

buy   build   building   built   plague   guess   guest   guide   guitar   guard

Section 8 — Silent h

which   what   when   where   why   while   white   wheel

Section 9 — Silent w

write   wrote   written   wreck   wrench   wrestling   wreath
wrap   wrong   two   who   whom   whose   whole

Section 10 — Silent gh

night   might   tight   light   lighten   delight   delighted
sight   fight   right   bright   brighten   fright   frighten
weight   eight   bought   brought   thought   caught   daughter

☐ My student has mastered the phonics words.   Tutor initials _____

Lesson 27 Spelling (page 1)
Special Spellings and Silent Letters

☐ Read the word list.   ☐ Read each word again and spell it aloud.

could	light	night	right	said	says
should	talk	they	walk	was	what
when	where	while	white	whole	would

☐ Write the word in your language.   ☐ Draw lines to match the words and sentences.
☐ Use the best English word to fill in the blanks.   ☐ Read the sentences aloud.

could _____   Some animals sleep during the day and hunt for food at _____.
light _____   I was happy I could give the _____ answer to my teacher.
night _____   All the cars have stopped, waiting for the _____ to turn green.
right _____   He asked if I _____ stay after the meeting and help clean up.
said _____   When I say, "Thank you, Mom", she always _____, "My pleasure!"
says _____   They _____ someone would come today and fix our broken window.

should _____   She will _____ to her boss and explain why she was late to work.
talk _____   You _____ go and visit your sick father.
they _____   I know _____ I want to do when my sister comes to visit.
walk _____   We will help them tomorrow if _____ will help us today.
was _____   Let's all _____ in together and sing "Happy Birthday" to her.
what _____   In the past he _____ sad and alone, but now things are different.

when _____   Can you tell me _____ your brother lives?
where _____   I was working _____ you were sleeping.
while _____   Do you know _____ the bus will arrive here?
white _____   If I had a bike, I _____ let you use it.
whole _____   Those four children ate a _____ watermelon!
would _____   In the old days, a nurse's uniform was usually _____.

☐ Checked by Tutor   Tutor initials _____

Lesson 27 Spelling (page 2)
Special Spellings and Silent Letters

> ☐ Read all the words. ☐ Write the best word under each picture.

bear	climb	thumb	elephants	lamb	wrench
building	comb	eight	guitar	women	write

_____   _____   _____   _____

_____   _____   _____   _____

_____   _____   _____   _____

Spelling Test: ☐ Practice the following words until you have learned them.

1. could	4. right	7. should	10. walk	13. when	16. white
2. light	5. said	8. talk	11. was	14. where	17. whole
3. night	6. says	9. they	12. what	15. while	18. would

☐ My student can spell these words aloud. Tutor Initials _____

☐ My student can write these words when I read them. Tutor Initials _____

Lesson 27 Sight Words

☐ Write the word in your language.
☐ Practice reading the words until you can pronounce them correctly.

amazed	captain	definite
direction	honest	immediately
innocent	lighten	might
question	reason	repent
result	royal	sailor
swallow	terrified	threw
throne	ticket	various
violent	world	worse

☐ My student can read these words and knows their meanings.   Tutor Initials _____

Lesson 27 – Use Sight & Spelling Words

☐ Read the sentences.   ☐ Draw lines to match the words and pictures.

There is a reason that sailor is climbing up
the mast of his ship.

She looks absolutely terrified!

That building looks like it might be a home or
fort for a royal family.

The reason there are so many microphones is because
we have reporters from various organizations.

I'm not sure who that man is, but he's right there
in his usual spot on the shore, reading a newspaper.

When the king is seated on his throne,
this servant will carry in the royal crown.

Those headphones also have a microphone.

You would be amazed how that machine can
lift a whole stack of logs at once.

He threw a ball that he knew his dog could catch.

When he puts his ticket into the slot,
the result is that the bar will lift and
allow his car to move ahead.

The king is wearing his royal robes.

She says she has a definite reason for bringing
these various sewing supplies.

☐ My student can read and understand these sentences. Tutor initials _____   53

Story 27 ◆ Jonah

☐ Read or listen to the story in your native language. Jonah 1:1-17; Jonah 3:1-10
☐ Find and mark the sight words in the story.   ☐ Listen to the story in English.

amazed
captain
definitely
direction
honestly
immediately
innocent
lighten
might
question
reason
repented
result
royal
sailors
swallowed
terrified
threw
throne
ticket
various
violent
world
worse

NOTE
"Casting lots" is something like drawing straws, rolling dice, or flipping a coin.

The Lord said to the prophet, Jonah, "I want you to go and preach at Nineveh. Tell them I'm going to destroy their city because of their evil ways."

Jonah knew that God would forgive the people of Nineveh if they repented. But those people were enemies of Israel, and Jonah didn't want to help them. Therefore, he went in a different direction, to another part of the world. At the seaport town of Joppa, he bought a ticket and got on a ship.

Once the ship was out at sea, God sent a violent storm. The sailors were terrified because the storm was about to break up their ship! They threw their cargo overboard in order to lighten the load. All the sailors started praying to their various gods; but Jonah was asleep down inside the ship.

The captain went and woke him up. He said, "How can you sleep? We are about to die! Get up and pray to your god."

Finally, the sailors began to think that this storm may have come upon them because of one certain person on the ship. They cast lots to see who it might be. The result showed that Jonah was definitely the reason for their trouble. They began to question him, "Who are you, and what have you done?"

Jonah answered their questions honestly. He said, "I serve the Lord God who made the sea and the dry ground; but I'm running away from him."

The sailors asked, "What should we do?"

Jonah said, "If you throw me overboard, the storm will definitely stop."

The men didn't want to kill an innocent man, so they worked hard to fight the storm; but it only grew worse. Finally, they realized they couldn't fight against God. They cried out to the Lord and asked him to forgive them for what they were about to do. At last, they took hold of Jonah and threw him overboard. Immediately, the storm stopped. The men were amazed! They bowed down, worshiped the Lord, and promised to serve only the one true God.

God had prepared a huge fish that swallowed Jonah as he fell into the water. After three days, Jonah prayed, "I will do what you want me to do." Then the Lord spoke to the fish and it vomited Jonah out onto the shore.

After that experience, Jonah obeyed God. He went to Nineveh. When he arrived, he began walking through the city. He shouted, "God is going to destroy this city in 40 days!"

All the people of Nineveh repented. Even the king came down from his throne and took off his royal robes. He prayed and fasted and told everyone else to do the same. He said, "God might change his mind and allow us to live."

The Lord saw all they were doing, and he knew they had turned away from their evil ways; so he did not destroy the huge city of Nineveh after all. Many thousands of people were spared because they repented after hearing the preaching of Jonah.

☐ Read the Story in English.   Tutor initials _____

Review Story 27

Use the words in the boxes to fill in the blanks.

| direction | lighten | repented | terrified | threw | ticket | violent | world |

1. Jonah knew that God would forgive the people of Nineveh if they _____.
2. Jonah didn't want to help them, therefore he went in a different _____, to another part of the _____. At Joppa, he bought a _____ and got on a ship.
3. Once the ship was out at sea, God sent a _____ storm. The sailors were _____ because the storm was about to break up their ship!
4. They _____ their cargo overboard in order to _____ the load.

| captain | definitely | honestly | question | reason | result | sailors | various |

5. All the sailors started praying to their _____ gods, but Jonah was asleep.
6. The _____ went and woke him up. He said, "Get up and pray to your god."
7. Finally, the _____ began to think that this storm may have come upon them because of one certain person on the ship. They cast lots to see who it might be. The _____ showed that Jonah was definitely the _____ for their trouble.
8. They began to _____ him, "Who are you, and what have you done?"
9. Jonah answered their questions _____. He said, "I serve the Lord God who made the sea and dry ground; but I'm running away from him." The sailors asked, "What should we do?"
10. Jonah said, "If you throw me overboard, the storm will _____ stop."

| amazed | Immediately | innocent | might | repented | royal | swallowed | throne | worse |

11. The men didn't want to kill an _____ man, so they worked hard to fight the storm; but it only grew _____. At last, they took hold of Jonah and threw him overboard.
12. _____, the storm stopped. The men were _____!
13. God had prepared a huge fish that _____ Jonah as he fell into the water. After three days, Jonah prayed, "I will do what you want me to do." Then the Lord spoke to the fish and it vomited Jonah out onto the shore.
14. All the people of Nineveh repented. Even the king came down from his _____ and took off his _____ robes. He prayed and fasted and told everyone else to do the same.
15. He said, "God _____ change his mind and allow us to live."
16. Many thousands of people were spared because they _____ after hearing the preaching of Jonah.

Read the sentences aloud. Tell the story in your own words. Tutor initials _____

Vocabulary 27 - What are they thinking or saying?

☐ Read the sentences.   ☐ Draw lines to match words and pictures.

I'm not thinking about anything definite.
I'm just sitting here enjoying the sunlight, while
various thoughts go through my mind.

I would help you if I could, but I honestly can't.
The reason is because I'm busy.

Listen to what this book says.
You need to repent!

I'm trying to think of
the answer to that question.

As a captain, there is no place I'd rather be
than at the wheel of my ship.

You should come immediately!
In two minutes you will be 'on air'.

I definitely know the answer to that question!

I hope this cough doesn't get any worse.

Is this the place where we turn in our tickets?

Things are a lot worse than I thought.

The reason I think of this as <u>my</u> calf is
because I was there when it was being born.

Right this way! Walk this direction.

56   ☐ Checked by Tutor   Tutor initials _____

Lesson 28

Phonics Word Reading

The /oo/ sound may be spelled oo, ew, o, wo, oe

☐ Practice reading the phonics words until you have mastered them.

Section 1 — Making the /oo/ sound with oo

too	boo	boot	boom	broom	room
groom	zoo	loom	bloom	gloom	gloomy
coop	scoop	loop	troop	stoop	droop
boot	hoot	shoot	school	food	noon
cool	pool	tool	stool	fool	foolish
soon	moon	spoon	balloon	tooth	booth
proof	loose	goose	moose	smooth	choose

Section 2 — Making the /oo/ sound with ew

blew	brew	crew	drew	grew	dew
few	flew	view	threw	chew	chewy
stew	cashew	jewel	knew	new	news

Section 3 — Making the /oo/ sound with o, wo, oe

do   to   two   who   canoe   lose   prove   move   movement

Section 4 — More words with oo & ew

caboose   papoose   kangaroo   raccoon   rooster   poodle   noodles

shampoo   toothpaste   toothbrush   toothpick   toothache

waterproof   rustproof   soundproof   fireproof

newspaper   newborn   newcomer   newlywed

☐ My student has mastered the phonics words.   Tutor initials _____

Lesson 28 Spelling (page 1)

Words having the /oo/ sound spelled with oo ew o

☐ Read the word list.   ☐ Read each word again and spell it aloud.

choose	do	few	food	grew	knew
move	new	noon	room	school	soon
threw	through	to	too	two	who

☐ Write the word in your language.   ☐ Draw lines to match the words and sentences.
☐ Use the best English word to fill in the blanks.   ☐ Read the sentences aloud.

choose _____   Don't just stand there and watch; ___ something to help!
do   _____   I can give you strawberry or chocolate; you _____.
few   _____   He _____ up in the north, but now he lives in the south.
food   _____   If you can find a _____ dry leaves, we can start our campfire.
grew   _____   The old woman says she _____ my parents when they were children.
knew   _____   Everyone will bring _____ to share at the potluck dinner.

---

move   _____   Let's start our meeting at _____ and then have lunch at one o'clock
new   _____   We can _____ over and make room for one more person at the table.
noon   _____   That child is thankful to have a _____ pencil with a good eraser.
room   _____   I just received her text. It says, "I'll see you _____."
school _____   Our English class meets in _____ 602.
soon   _____   The children are at _____ every day until three in the afternoon.

---

threw   _____   Do you know _____ is coming to supper this evening?
through _____   I have a way ___ work this morning, but I'll need a ride home tonight
to   _____   I'm so sorry! I thought it was trash, and I _____ it away.
too   _____   There was deep water on the road, and they couldn't get _____
two   _____   I am _____ tired to study tonight, but I will do it in the morning.
who   _____   I have _____ pens, so I will let you use one of them.

☐ Checked by Tutor   Tutor initials _____

Lesson 28 Spelling (page 2)

The /oo/ sound may be spelled oo, ew, o, wo, oe

☐ Read all the words.   ☐ Write the best word under each picture.

| boot | goose | newspaper | room | two | tools |
| broom | kangaroo | raccoon | rooster | stew | cartoon |

kangaroo   raccoon   rooster   goose

room   tools   broom   newspaper

boot   two   stew   cartoon

Spelling Test: ☐ Practice the following words until you have learned them.

1. choose   4. food   7. move   10. room   13. threw   16. too
2. do   5. grew   8. new   11. school 14. through 17. two
3. few   6. knew   9. noon   12. soon   15. to   18. who

☐ My student can spell these words aloud. Tutor Initials _____

☐ My student can write these words when I read them. Tutor Initials _____

Lesson 28 Sight Words

☐ Write the word in your language.
☐ Practice reading the words until you can pronounce them correctly.

among	begin	captive
chose	court	easily
education	event	furious
furnace	gather	government
high	include	music
occasion	official	position
rescue	shocked	special
themselves	usual	whenever

☐ My student can read these words and knows their meanings.   Tutor Initials _____

Lesson 28 – Use Sight & Spelling Words

☐ Read the sentences. ☐ Draw lines to match the words and pictures.

He is shocked to find the safe open
and his money gone.

She chose her usual spot on that high stool
where she likes to sit and prepare food.

With this special kind of bed, you can
easily move a sleeping baby from one room
to another whenever you choose.

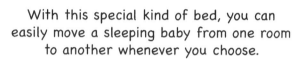

Whenever a new business opens, a government
official comes for the special event, and
they have a "ribbon-cutting" ceremony.

Those tigers were taken captive, and they now
live in a zoo. They can't get loose, but
they do have room to move around.

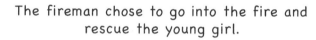

The fireman chose to go into the fire and
rescue the young girl.

That little child has a special chair
so he can sit higher at the table.

With two men in that canoe, they can
easily move on the water or even
through the reeds close to the shore.

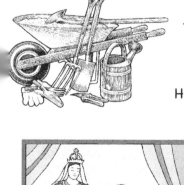

These garden tools were hidden among the stuff in
our storage building. We gathered them together
so you could choose which ones you will use.

He is down on one knee in the royal court, asking
for help with something he wants to do.

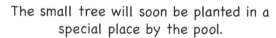

The small tree will soon be planted in a
special place by the pool.

The cow is chewing on hay made from
grass that grew last summer.

☐ My student can read and understand these sentences. Tutor initials _____

Story 28 ◆ The Fiery Furnace

☐ Read or listen to the story in your native language. Daniel 3:1-30

☐ Find and mark the sight words in the story.   ☐ Listen to the story in English.

among
begins
captive
chose
court
easily
education
event
furious
furnace
gathered
government
high
includes
music
occasion
officials
positions
rescue
shocked
special
themselves
usual
whenever

statue:
A sculpture (usually of a person or animal) made from wood, clay, stone, or metal.

Nebuchadnezzar was the king of Babylon. His army came through Jerusalem and took many people captive. He chose some of the best young men and took them away to Babylon where they had to study and get an education to serve in the king's court. Three of these were Shadrach, Meshach, and Abednego. Over the years, they grew stronger and wiser than the other men in the palace. God gave them knowledge and understanding. Whenever the king wanted advice, he talked to these men. He trusted them and gave them high positions in the government.

Some time later, Nebuchadnezzar made a statue of gold that was 90 feet high and nine feet wide. The king called together a large group of people for a special event to honor the statue. He ordered them, "When the music begins, bow down and worship the statue. If you don't obey this command, you'll be thrown into a burning, fiery furnace."

The music began, and all the people bowed low to the ground in front of the gold statue; that is, all except the three Jewish men. This occasion gave certain Babylonian officials a chance to get rid of some of the Jews that were among them. They said to the king, "There are three Jews in high positions in the kingdom who did not bow down to your statue. Their names are Shadrach, Meshach, and Abednego."

The king sent for the three men and told them that he would play the music again and give them a second chance. The king said, "Everyone has to bow down to my statue, and that includes you! If you don't bow down, you will be thrown into a burning, fiery furnace. No god can rescue you from my power."

The men answered the king. "Our God can easily rescue us from your power; but if he doesn't, we still won't worship the statue."

Nebuchadnezzar was furious! He commanded that the furnace be heated seven times hotter than usual. Then he ordered some of his strongest soldiers to tie up the three young men and throw them into it. But the furnace was so hot that the soldiers themselves were killed as they threw in the young men.

When the king looked into the fire, he was shocked! He jumped up and shouted, "Didn't we tie up three men and throw them into the fire?"

"Yes, Your Majesty. We threw in three men."

"I see four men walking around in there, and they're not tied up. Look! The form of the fourth man is like the Son of God."

Nebuchadnezzar came close to the furnace and shouted, "Shadrach, Meshach, Abednego, servants of the Most High God, come out!" As the men came out of the fire, everyone gathered around to see them. They were amazed that the men hadn't been hurt and didn't even have the smell of fire on them!

The king announced, "God sent his angel to rescue these men because they were willing to die rather than bow down to any other god. Now, if anyone says anything against the God of Israel, that person will be destroyed, and their house will be made into a trash heap."

☐ Read the Story in English.   Tutor initials _____

Review Story 28

Use the words in the boxes to fill in the blanks.

| captive | chose | court | education | government | high | Whenever |

1. Nebuchadnezzar's army came through Jerusalem and took many people _____.
2. He _____ some of the best young men, and took them away to Babylon where they had to study and get an _____ to serve in the king's _____.
3. Three of these were Shadrach, Meshach, and Abednego. God gave them knowledge and understanding. _____ the king wanted advice he talked to these men.
4. He trusted them and gave them high positions in the _____.
5. Nebuchadnezzar made a statue of gold that was 90 feet _____ and nine feet wide.

| among | begins | event | furnace | music | occasion | officials | positions | special |

6. The king called together a large group of people for a _____ _____.
7. He ordered them, "When the music _____, bow down and worship the statue.
8. If you don't obey this command, you'll be thrown into a burning, fiery _____."
9. The _____ began and the people bowed low to the ground in front of the gold statue.
10. This _____ gave certain Babylonian _____ a chance to get rid of some of the Jews that were _____ them. They told the king, "There are three Jews in high _____ in the kingdom who did not bow down to your statue."

| easily | furious | gathered | includes | rescue | shocked | themselves | usual |

11. The king said, "Everyone has to bow down to my statue, and that _____ you! No god can _____ you from my power."
12. The men answered the king, "Our God can _____ rescue us from your power; but if he doesn't, we still won't worship the statue."
13. Nebuchadnezzar was _____! He commanded that the furnace be heated seven times hotter than _____. The three young men were tied up. But the furnace was so hot that the soldiers _____ were killed as they threw in the young men.
14. When the king looked into the fire, he was _____! He said, "I see four men walking around in there. Look! The form of the fourth man is like the Son of God!"
15. As the men came out of the fire, everyone _____ around to see them. They were amazed that the men hadn't been hurt and didn't even have the smell of fire on them!

Vocabulary 28 ~ What are they thinking or saying?

☐ Read the sentences.   ☐ Draw lines to match words and pictures.

Some people like to see the news on TV or online,
but I'd rather read a newspaper.

I do want you to 'look your best'
for this special occasion.

I heard the news, and I'm
furious with you! Now leave!

I need to choose one toy to give my
baby sister, whenever she cries.

I need someone to help me with this microphone.
It is much too high for me!

I want to choose the best fruit I can find
for our special breakfast tomorrow.

As we begin our new school year,
I would like to introduce myself to you.

I threw away the old broom, but I can easily
make a new one. I have the tools to do so.

When I receive news that a
crowd has gathered outside our government office,
I have to 'take action'.

My father always said, "Education begins at home."

I knew I would see you around noon, because
it's your usual time to drive through.

Whenever we hear our special song begin,
we want to move in time to the music.

64   ☐ Checked by Tutor   Tutor initials _____

Lesson 29

Phonics Word Reading

The /aw/ sound may be spelled au & aw

☐ Practice reading the phonics words until you have mastered them.

Section 1 — The /aw/ sound spelled with au

audio	taught	caught	caution	cause	because
applaud	applause	fraud	faucet	fault	vault
pause	gauze	haul	haunt	laundry	August
launch	sausage	sauce	saucer	sauna	trauma
auction	audience	author	authority	auto	automobile

Section 2 — The /aw/ sound spelled with aw

jaw	law	paw	raw	saw	sawdust
claw	flaw	draw	drawing	withdraw	drawstring
shawl	thaw	outlaw	coleslaw	straw	strawberry
dawn	fawn	pawn	yawn	lawn	lawnmower
awl	crawl	awning	awful	hawk	squawk

☐ My student has mastered the phonics words.   Tutor initials _____

Lesson 29 Spelling (page 1)

The /aw/ sound spelled with au & aw

☐ Read the word list.   ☐ Read each word again and spell it aloud.

audience	auto	awful	because	caught	cause
caution	daughter	dawn	draw	fault	haul
launch	law	lawn	pause	straw	taught

☐ Write the word in your language.   ☐ Draw lines to match the words and sentences.
☐ Use the best English word to fill in the blanks.   ☐ Read the sentences aloud.

audience _____   After his car was in a wreck, he took it to an _____ body shop.
auto _____   They can't grow mangoes _____ they live in Alaska.
awful _____   I spoke loudly because the _____ was mostly older people.
because _____   Not having enough water can _____ your plants to die.
caught _____   He stayed in bed because he had a high fever and he felt _____.
cause _____   His shirt ripped when it got _____ on a thorn bush.

Caution _____   I will _____ a map that shows you the way to my house.
daughter _____   She likes to wake up before _____ and listen to the chirping of birds
dawn _____   The sign said, "_____, slippery when wet."
draw _____   It's your _____ if you get hurt when you don't obey a stop sign.
fault _____   That big semi truck can _____ several cars at once.
haul _____   Is that her younger sister or her _____?

launch _____   Our state has a _____ about wearing seat belts in a car.
law _____   Many different animals like to sleep on a bed of _____.
lawn _____   There are several good places to _____ a boat on this river.
pause _____   That young man _____ himself how to play guitar.
straw _____   He cuts the _____ short, so we can easily walk on the grass.
taught _____   When he tells a story, he likes to _____ before the last sentence

☐ Checked by Tutor   Tutor initials _____

Lesson 29 Spelling (page 2)

The /aw/ sound spelled with au & aw

☐ Read all the words.   ☐ Write the best word under each picture.

| audience | claws | faucet | hawk | lawn | audio |
| caught | draw | straw | laundry | yawn | caution |

Spelling Test: ☐ Practice the following words until you have learned them.

1. audience
2. auto
3. awful
4. because
5. caught
6. cause
7. caution
8. daughter
9. dawn
10. draw
11. fault
12. haul
13. launch
14. law
15. lawn
16. pause
17. straw
18. taught

☐ My student can spell these words aloud.   Tutor Initials _____

☐ My student can write these words when I read them.   Tutor Initials _____

67

Lesson 29 Sight Words

☐ Write the word in your language.
☐ Practice reading the words until you can pronounce them correctly.

ability	attitude	authority
cancel	concerned	create
effort	exactly	idea
jealous	language	miserable
mistake	moment	opportunity
provide	punishment	remove
respect	several	sign
suggest	supposed	totally

☐ My student can read these words and knows their meanings.   Tutor Initials _____

Lesson 29 – Use Sight & Spelling Words

☐ Read the sentences.   ☐ Draw lines to match the words and pictures.

The certificate will be signed by
the president of the college.

She has several ways to carry food and water.

If the animal lifts its paw for a moment,
the mouse can escape.

The paw prints might be those of a large dog.

We created that 'scarecrow' because
it was supposed to scare away birds from our
berry patch. But it doesn't work.

He's lying on the beach almost totally
covered with sand.

There are two straws in that drink.

He has an opportunity to suggest some ideas,
so he brought several plans.

Using his new lawn tractor, that man can
do several jobs with less effort than
it used to take to do one lawn.

That truck is supposed to be able to haul
extremely heavy loads.

They found fault with him because
he paused from his work and prayed to God.

The bear just caught a fish.

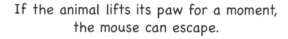
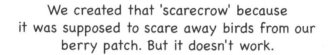
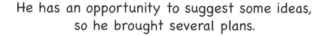

☐ My student can read and understand these sentences.   Tutor initials _____

Story 29 ◆ Daniel and the Den of Lions

☐ Read or listen to the story in your native language. Daniel 6:1-28
☐ Find and mark the sight words in the story. ☐ Listen to the story in English.

ability
attitude
authority
canceled
concerned
create
effort
exactly
idea
jealous
languages
miserable
mistake
moment
opportunity
provided
punishment
remove
respected
Several
sign
suggested
supposed
totally

Daniel was a young Jewish man who was captured in Jerusalem and taken away to Babylon. There he served in the king's court through the time of many kings. Over the years, Daniel became highly respected, and he was given great authority. King Darius had three main government officials, but Daniel was his favorite. He had the most ability of them all, and he did everything he was supposed to do.

Daniel's work and his attitude were so good that the king was planning to make him the head officer over the whole kingdom. Several of the other men were jealous, so they suggested an idea that was sure to get Daniel in trouble. They went to the king and said, "Oh, King, live forever! We have thought of a way to honor you. Please create a law that says no one can pray to any god except you for 30 days. Anyone who disobeys this law will be thrown into the den of lions." The king liked the idea, so he made the law.

Daniel heard about the new law, but still, three times a day he went into his room and opened the window that faced Jerusalem. There he prayed and worshiped God in the same way as before. This was exactly what the other men knew Daniel would do, and it provided just the opportunity they were looking for. They asked the king, "Didn't you sign a law that says no one can pray to any god except you, or they will be thrown into a den of lions?"

"Yes, I did. In fact, I made it a special law that can't be changed."

"Oh, king, it makes us sad to tell you that Daniel, a Jew, is breaking that law. He prays and worships his God three times a day."

Suddenly, the king knew he had made a terrible mistake! He wanted very much to protect Daniel, and he worked with great effort to find a way to change the law; but it couldn't be done.

Daniel was put into the lions' den, and a huge stone with the king's seal was placed over the opening so that no one could stop the punishment.

The king was miserable! He went back to his palace and canceled all his plans for the evening. He was so concerned about Daniel that he didn't eat or sleep all night.

In the morning, he rushed to the lions' den and ordered the guards to remove the stone. The king cried loudly, "Oh, Daniel, servant of the Most High God, was your God able to save you from the lions?"

Daniel called back to him, "Oh, King, live forever! My God sent his angel to shut the mouths of the lions. I have not been hurt in any way." With joy, the king gave the order to have Daniel brought up out of the lions' den.

The king then ordered his guards. "Go get those men who came up with this idea against Daniel, and throw them all into the den of lions."

It was done exactly as the king commanded. The moment those men were thrown in, the lions were waiting at the bottom of the pit and ripped them apart before they ever reached the floor!

King Darius wrote a totally new law and sent it out to people of all languages in his kingdom. He said, "Everyone is to fear Daniel's God because he is the living God. His kingdom will last forever, and he is able to save those who serve him."

☐ Read the Story in English.   Tutor initials _____

Review Story 29

Use the words in the boxes to fill in the blanks.

| ability | attitude | authority | jealous | respected | Several | supposed |

1. Daniel became highly _____, and he was given great _____.
2. King Darius had three main government officials, but Daniel was his favorite. He had the most _____ of them all, and he did everything he was _____ to do.
3. Daniel's work and his _____ were so good that the king was planning to make him the head officer over the whole kingdom.
4. _____ of the other men were _____.

| create | effort | mistake | opportunity | provided | punishment | sign | suggested |

5. They _____ an idea that was sure to get Daniel in trouble. They said to the king, "Please _____ a law that says no one can pray to any god except you for 30 days."
6. Daniel heard about the new law, but he still worshiped God in the same way as before. This was exactly what the other men knew Daniel would do, and it _____ just the _____ they were looking for. They asked the king, "Didn't you _____ a law that says no one can pray to any god except you, or they will be thrown into a den of lions?"
7. Suddenly, the king knew he had made a terrible _____!
8. He worked with great _____ to find a way to change the law, but it couldn't be done.
9. Daniel was put into the lions' den, and a huge stone with the king's seal was placed over the opening so that no one could stop the _____.

| canceled | concerned | exactly | idea | languages | moment | remove | totally | miserable |

10. The king was _____! He went back to his palace and _____ all his plans for the evening. He was so _____ about Daniel that he didn't eat or sleep all night.
11. In the morning, he rushed to the lions' den, ordered the guards to _____ the stone, and found that Daniel was safe.
12. The king then ordered his guards, "Go get those men who came up with this _____ against Daniel, and throw them all into the den of lions." It was done _____ as the king commanded. The _____ those men were thrown in, the lions were waiting at the bottom of the pit and ripped them apart before they ever reached the floor!
13. King Darius wrote a _____ new law and sent it out to people of all _____ in his kingdom. It said, "Everyone is to fear Daniel's God because he is the living God. His kingdom will last forever, and he is able to save those who serve him."

Read the sentences aloud.   Tell the story in your own words.   Tutor initials _____

Vocabulary 29 – What are they thinking or saying?

☐ Read the sentences. ☐ Draw lines to match words and pictures.

I'm concerned about you. Is something wrong?

I looked at several pieces of wood, and this one 'caught my eye'. It's exactly what I need to create that shelf that's supposed to go in our workroom.

That's what I was afraid of. I see several mistakes in here. I'm glad we 'caught that mistake' before printing any more copies.

I'm so happy for this opportunity to sit in the audience with my grandfather!

This is my favorite shawl, and I wear it as a sign of respect.

I'm going to draw some flowers and create a beautiful card for my teacher.

I feel miserable, but I've taken some medicine that's supposed to help.

With great effort, I have the ability to make the audience feel that my 'dummy' is talking.

I was taught to be cheerful and try to see good in every situation.

Each evening I pause and give thanks because God provided exactly the son I always dreamed of!

Don't be concerned. I caught myself, and I didn't hit my head.

I don't have the ability to fix this. We can no longer get parts for these old machines.

☐ Checked by Tutor   Tutor initials _____

Lesson 30
Phonics Word Reading

Words with oi & oy

☐ Practice reading the Phonics Words until you have mastered them.

Section 1 — words containing oi

oil	oiled	oiling	oily	coil	coiled
boil	boiled	boiling	boiler	broil	choice
foil	soil	soiled	spoil	spoiled	toil
toilet	coin	void	avoid	noise	noisy
join	joined	joint	point	appoint	anoint
poised	voice	invoice	oink	groin	sirloin
rejoice	hoist	moist	moisture	moisten	poison

Section 2 — words containing oy

coy	toy	soy	soybean	destroy	destroyer
joy	enjoy	joyful	joyfully	joyous	joyride
loyal	loyalty	royal	royalty	oyster	voyage
boy	boyish	boyhood	tomboy	busboy	cowboy
annoy	deploy	employ	employer	employee	employment

Section 3 — More words with oi & oy

pinpoint   ballpoint   viewpoint   checkpoint

ointment   appointment   disappoint

enjoyable   enjoyment

☐ My student has mastered the phonics words.   Tutor initials _____

Lesson 30 Spelling (page 1)

Words with oi & oy

☐ Read the word list.   ☐ Read each word again and spell it aloud.

boil	boy	choice	enjoy	join	joint
joy	loyal	moist	noise	oil	point
poison	royal	soil	spoil	toy	voice

☐ Write the word in your language.   ☐ Draw lines to match the words and sentences.
☐ Use the best English word to fill in the blanks.   ☐ Read the sentences aloud.

boil　_____　　I hope we have a _____ about which day we get off.

boy　_____　　It would be a good idea to _____ that water before drinking it.

choice_____　　When he was a _____, he had to work very hard.

enjoy_____　　Let's _____ together and buy a gift for our teacher.

join　_____　　A slow walk might help to lessen the pain in your hip _____.

joint　_____　　You will _____ reading this note from your grandmother.

---

joy　_____　　That plant grows best in soil that is _____ but not too wet.

loyal_____　　Mom says she likes to hear the _____ of happy children.

moist_____　　I am filled with _____ when I think about our visit yesterday.

noise_____　　Be careful with the _____ of your pencil.

oil　_____　　They are _____ to their teacher and will obey her wishes.

point_____　　Spread a little _____ in the pan when you fry the potatoes.

---

poison_____　　There are things you can do to help your garden have better _____.

royal_____　　We learned about the king and other people in the _____ family.

soil　_____　　They didn't realize that the beautiful plant had _____ leaves.

spoil_____　　The best birthday gift he can remember was a _____ train.

toy　_____　　Something I will always love is the sound of my mother's _____.

voice_____　　If you use too much salt, it will _____ the taste of your soup.

74　　　☐ Checked by Tutor　　Tutor initials _____

Lesson 30 Spelling (page 2)
Words with oi & oy

☐ Read all the words.   ☐ Write the best word under each picture.

boil	coin	noise	oink	poison	soil
boy	cowboy	oil rig	point	rejoice	toy

Spelling Test: ☐ Practice the following words until you have learned them.

1. boil
2. boy
3. choice
4. enjoy
5. join
6. joint
7. joy
8. loyal
9. moist
10. noise
11. oil
12. point
13. poison
14. royal
15. soil
16. spoil
17. toy
18. voice

☐ My student can spell these words aloud.   Tutor Initials _____

☐ My student can write these words when I read them.   Tutor Initials _____

Lesson 30 Sight Words

☐ Write the word in your language.
☐ Practice reading the words until you can pronounce them correctly.

action	banquet	custom
decision	determined	discover
enemy	entire	excellent
goes	horrified	horse
important	information	meant
mercy	nothing	probably
record	report	request
responsible	reward	yesterday

☐ My student can read these words and knows their meanings.   Tutor Initials _____

Lesson 30 – Use Sight & Spelling Words

❏ Read the sentences. ❏ Draw lines to match the words and pictures.

She feels important as she goes to her office each day.

That is an old custom for weddings.

He just discovered a valuable stone.

He's enjoying a nap in a hammock with his feet up.

It's empty! There's nothing in that box.

If you want to request a song, he can probably play it for you.

Those important papers are kept in a safe place.

He is writing a report. It will go into the official record book.

That pet always gets a reward for doing his tricks.

His umbrella has been ruined by the wind.

That used to be a beautiful tower. Now it is in ruins.

The servant is leading a horse through the streets.

❏ My student can read and understand these sentences.   Tutor initials _____

Story 30 ◆ Esther

☐ Read or listen to the story in your native language.

Esther 2:5-10; Esther 2:21-23; Esther 3:1-15; Esther 5:1-14; Esther 6:1-14; Esther 7:1-10

☐ Find and mark the sight words in the story.   ☐ Listen to the story in English.

action
banquet
customs
decision
determined
discovered
enemy
entire
excellent
goes
horrified
horse
important
information
meant
mercy
nothing
probably
record
reported
request
responsible
reward
yesterday

gallows: A structure made for hanging a person who has been sentenced to death.

Mordecai was a Jew who worked at the palace of the King of Persia. He had a young relative named Esther. After both her parents died, he became like a father to her. At that time, the King of Persia was looking for a new queen. He brought many beautiful young women to his palace, and Esther was among them. Mordecai told her not to tell anyone she was Jewish. When the king made his choice, Esther became the new queen.

While Mordecai was at work, he discovered a plot to kill the king. He reported the information, and his good deed was written in the palace record book.

A man named Haman was second in command to the king. When he walked by, everyone bowed low, except Mordecai. Haman was angry! He told the king, "The Jews have customs that are against your laws. They should all be killed." So the order was sent out to the entire kingdom that all Jewish people would be killed on a certain day.

Mordecai heard about the order and sent a message to Esther: "Talk to the king and beg him to have mercy on you and your people. You need to take action! It may be that you have come to the kingdom for such a time as this."

After three days, Esther made her decision. She put on her royal robes and went to the king's court. The king was happy to see her. He said, "Tell me your request, and I will give it to you—even up to half my kingdom."

She answered, "I want you and Haman to come to my banquet this evening."

The king and Haman went to her banquet and, while they were at the table, the king said, "Tell me your request so I can give it to you."

She said, "You and Haman come to my banquet tomorrow. Then I will tell you my request." As Haman left, he felt important and proud. He had been invited to the queen's banquet two days in a row! Then Mordecai again refused to bow down to him. Haman's joy was ruined, and he was determined to get rid of Mordecai. That evening, he built a 75-foot gallows at his house and planned to hang Mordecai on it the next day.

That same night, the king couldn't sleep, so he asked a servant to read to him from the palace record book. The servant read how Mordecai was responsible for saving the king's life. The king asked, "What was done to reward him?"

The servant answered, "Nothing."

"Nothing?! Go and see who is in the outer court." There the servant found Haman. The king said, "Bring him in." Before Haman could speak, the king asked him, "What should be done for a man that the king wants to honor?" Haman thought, *The king probably means me.* So he answered, "If you really want to honor a man, dress him in one of your robes and a crown. Put him on your best horse. As he goes through the streets, have someone go ahead of him shouting, 'This is what the king does for the man he wants to honor.'"

The king replied, "Excellent idea! Go find Mordecai and do just what you have said." Haman was horrified! This meant he had to honor the man he hated; but he did it. When he finished, he had just enough time to make it to the queen's banquet.

After the meal, the king once again said to Esther, "Now, tell me your request."

Esther said, "Please spare our lives. A man has ordered me and my people destroyed."

The king asked, "What man has done this, and where is he?"

Esther pointed at Haman. "Our enemy is that wicked man." Haman was so terrified, he couldn't even speak! One of the servants told the king, "Yesterday, Haman built a 75-foot gallows on which to hang the man who saved your life."

The king was furious! He ordered, "Hang Haman on his own gallows." So it was, that the Jewish people were rescued. Haman was dead, and his job was given to Mordecai.

☐ Read the Story in English.   Tutor initials _____

Review Story 30

Use the words in the boxes to fill in the blanks.

| action   customs   decision   discovered   entire   information   mercy   reported   request |

1. While Mordecai was at work, he _____ a plot to kill the king. He _____ the _____, and his good deed was written in the palace record book.
2. Haman told the king, "The Jews have _____ that are against your laws. They should all be killed." So the order was sent out to the _____ kingdom.
3. Mordecai sent a message to Esther: "Talk to the king and beg him to have _____ on you and your people. You need to take _____!"
4. Esther made her _____. She put on her royal robes and went to the king's court. The king said, "Tell me your _____ and I will give it to you—even up to half my kingdom."

| banquet   determined   important   Nothing   record   responsible   reward |

5. She answered, "I want you and Haman to come to my _____ this evening." That evening Esther invited the king and Haman to another banquet the following day.
6. As Haman left, he felt _____ and proud. Then Mordecai again refused to bow down to him. Haman's joy was ruined, and he was _____ to get rid of Mordecai.
7. That night, the king asked a servant to read to him from the palace _____ book.
8. The servant read how Mordecai was _____ for saving the king's life. The king asked, "What was done to _____ him?" The servant answered, "_____."

| enemy   Excellent   goes   horrified   horse   meant   probably   Yesterday |

9. The king asked Haman, "What should be done for a man that the king wants to honor?" Haman thought, *The king _____ means me.* So he answered, "If you really want to honor a man, dress him in one of your robes and a crown. Put him on your best _____.
10. As he _____ through the streets, have someone go ahead of him shouting, 'This is what the king does for the man he wants to honor.'"
11. The king replied, "_____ idea! Go find Mordecai and do everything just as you have said." Haman was _____! This _____ he had to honor the man he hated; but he did it.
12. Esther said, "A man has ordered me and my people destroyed." The king asked, "What man has done this, and where is he?" Esther pointed at Haman. "Our _____ is that wicked man!"
13. One of the servants told the king, "_____, Haman built a 75-foot gallows on which to hang the man who saved your life." The king ordered, "Hang Haman on his own gallows!"

Read the sentences aloud.   Tell the story in your own words.   Tutor initials _____

Vocabulary 30 – What are they thinking or saying?

❑ Read the sentences.   ❑ Draw lines to match words and pictures.

I received an excellent grade!

I hate to give you this ticket, but I have no choice.
Our chief ordered us to take action and
not show any mercy at this point.

If you need to know anything, just ask me.
I enjoy helping people!

I can't believe you spilled your coffee
and ruined my report!

I've discovered that music is an excellent way
to bring joy to myself and to others.

You made a good decision to ride in my taxi.
I know every street in this entire city!

I like having Dad as my horse.

I'm so happy, I can't help 'jumping for joy.'

This is my favorite toy. I like the red color
and I like the noise it makes.

Come on! You took a step yesterday and
I'm determined you will do it again today!

If you want to enjoy an excellent cup of tea,
first, pour boiling water into the teapot to
heat it up. Then make your tea.

Nothing brings me more joy than
the love my child shows me.

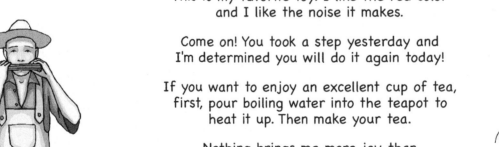

❑ Checked by Tutor   Tutor initials _____

Certificate of Achievement

My student, _____

has completed all the lessons in

Language Olympics
English Language Learning - Book 3

Congratulations!

Tutor Signature _____

Date _____

Our Mission
Sharing the story of God for discipleship using all the stories of the Bible.

Our Websites
BibleTelling.org – all BibleTelling news, events, and services (including Seminars in Israel, Training, and free download of All the Stories of the Bible)
BTStories.com – free online access to audio, video, text, timeline, map, and insights for *All the Stories of the Bible*
ChristianStorytelling.com – official website of the annual conference
LanguageOlympics.org – literacy and ESL training using 60 Bible stories

Our Media and Resources
YouTube video series: https://bit.ly/2rLOZFY – The Art of Storytelling
Amazon books/ebooks: https://amzn.to/2j7LER2 – Author page for John Walsh
Amazon books/ebooks: https://amzn.to/2Tpzcup – Author page for Jan Walsh

Story of the Day Subscription
Receive an e-mail each weekday with links to the video, audio, and narrative of the story of the day.
E-mail your subscription request to **info@BibleTelling.com**.

Facebook
Search for "BibleTelling"

Mobile App
Search for "BT Stories" in the Apple, Android, and Windows app stores

Contact
E-mail us at info@BibleTelling.com with any questions.

Post comments or questions on our Facebook page.

BibleTelling
2905 Gill Street
Bloomington, IL 61704

Made in the USA
Middletown, DE
07 March 2023

26362068R00051